# A GIFT III

## LUZVIMINDA G. RIVERA

Foreword by Shiju H. Pallithazheth
Edited by Ayo Gutierrez
Illustrator:  Kenneth Furnace
Cover Design: GMGA Publishing

# TABLE OF CONTENTS


Acknowledgment     5
Foreword     7
Introduction     10
Reviews     14
**Prelude to Love**     20
    Amore Mio     21
**On Friendship and Love**     39
    Because of Your Love
    Drifted Into Paradise
    How Did I Fall In Love
    I Will Live For You
    Joy To My Heart
    Love in Multi Task
    None Like You
    Promise! You Will Hold Me In Your Life
    Querencia
    Saudade
    Serendipity
    The Heart Will Never Forget
    Tonight the Moon Laughs
    To You I Promise
    You Are Everything
**On Pain and Loss**     56
    A Day Without You
    Beginning To Its End
    Butterfly And Its Broken Wings
    Broken
    Elusive Fate
    Far Away

If I Ask You
Reaching Out
Spirits Lament
Tonight Her Tears Fall
Verses of Life
When Goodbye Is Not Forever

**On Inspiration, Hopes and Dreams**          72
Beautiful India
Beyond My Limits
For How Long
Hear Our Prayers
I Need You
In Everything
Life's Essence
Metanoia
Only You And Me
Metaphor (Acrostic)
When The Seagulls Fly
You Are My Everything
Your Promises

**Translation to Philippines Languages.**     95-116
A Gift 1 5 Series
Pangasinense
Tagalog

**Translation to International Languages.**  117-202
A Gift 1 5 Series
Albanian (Albania - Europe
Assamese (India - Asia)
Bengali     (India – Asia)
Brazilian.  (Brazil-Europe)
Dari        (Afghanistan –Asia)
Gujarati    (India – Asia)

Pashto       (Afghanistan —Asia)
Punjab.     (India — Asia)
Setswana.   (Africa- Asia)
Tamil.       (India — Asia)
Vietnamese (Vietnam-Asia)
Dedicated Poem                                      203
A Gift: Music Piece                                 217
About the Author                                    221
Translators of the Philippine Languages             224
Translators of International Languages              227
About the Editor                                    239
About the Illustrator                               241
About the Music Artist                              243
About Hon. Shiju H. Pallithazheth                   246
About Corina Junghiatu                              247
About the Reviewers                                 248
Invitation                                          255

# ACKNOWLEDGMENT

The author gratefully acknowledges all those who have extended their time, effort, most valuable guidance, encouragement, and assistance that contributed to this book's realization.

To everybody who had been "A Gift "in this journey that inspires the author to pursue book III, here's my utmost gratitude.

I express my utmost respect and gratitude to Honorable Shiju H. Pallithazheth for the excellent foreword and Corina Junghiatu for the beautiful introduction of the book.

A Gift III is our gift to the world. I thank my translators, who are also prominent poets of their countries for their good heart in voluntarily translating my poem, A GIFT, in five sequels to their languages. The Philippine language translators are John-John J. Flores (Pangasinense) and  Zaldy F. Perez ( Tagalog). For the International languages translators namely: Sherife Allko (Albanian), Malakshimi Borthakur (Assamese), Queen Sarkar (Bengali), Shakil Kalam (Brazilian),  Parwez Hashimi ( Dar and Pashto)  Bhanubai Patel (Gujarati), Mohit Katyal (Punjabi), Kenneth Maswabi (Setswana), K. Radhakrishnan (Tamil),  Ram  Krishna  Perugu (Telugo) and Nguyen Chinch Vietnamese).

To my excellent reviewers: Magie F-V-Vijay Kumar, William Thomas Fearby, Shailesh Gupta Veer, K.Radhakrishnan, Liza Joy Tomey, and Jyoti Nair, please accept my humble appreciation.

Kudos to Ayo Gutierrez for successfully editing the A Gift series.

I won't fail to mention  Kenneth Furnace, my creative illustrator and Noven Perez, the A Gift music artist.

This book is my tribute to "A Gift" who has inspired my writing journey.

Most of all, to the ALMIGHTY GOD, the source of her strength and wisdom, who made everything possible.

# FOREWORD

Poetry is a gift nurtured by some blessed souls to amuse and clean the society from thoughts that stain. It needs a cosmic approach where the poet decides to put his or her heart in an honest and gratifying manner giving tribute to the cosmic world. The poet takes time to purge his or her thoughts only to retain relevance so that the sage literary human within him or her emerge. That is the real poet. The element of realization becomes productive once a poet manages to succeed in doing that. He or she is endowed with the cosmic gift, which could provoke the readers to think and get influenced. The verses remain grounded but relaying powerful messages that become relevant to society and give them a relief to heal. That is poetry.

This book, *A Gift III* carries forward the legacy from the former two Amazon bestsellers, *A Gift I* and *A Gift II*. The prolific Author Luzviminda Gabato Rivera keeps her pen charged and inspired in this book with five gift poems translated to 14 languages. Author Luzviminda has gone beyond the translated version and added additional literary maverick of 40 poems in free verse from her. So, isn't that a treasure finds of a summed up hundred and ten poems? Yes, author Luzviminda has her perception of love, friendship, pain, hopes, dreams, and inspiration bonded and summed up in *A Gift III*. It does assure value to the human bond and gets the reader to embark on unexpected revelations. A book is read to feed sagacity to every nativity. When it comes to the nativity in the world of literature, it connects all as one world. This book has been influential in showing justice to that deep thought and will be a book that you will find difficult to let go of before its completion.

As a successful global poet, her acumen and potentials prompt me to write a humble tribute to her in this foreword.

I have seen you come as a bud,
Today you are far ahead.

You are a bloomed garden,
And one who can never be forgotten.

Poetry runs through your veins,
Your golden pen speaks for it by all means.

Keep your literary journey similar,
The world today knows you as one familiar.

Luzviminda, look back to when you started as a bud,
You'll realize, today you're never the same head.

Your poetic thoughts have advanced today,
And it's sure to develop further every day.

Keep the flood of thoughts pouring,

It's your gesture to the world, as one caring.
The Gift III speaks sense, fantasy, imageries, and cosmic blessings. See it all for yourself before I sum it all up in this foreword to break the suspense. I wouldn't break the suspense for sure and will leave you, readers, to find it on your own. Feel the treasure and start flipping the pages

## Shiju H. Pallithazheth
Best Selling Author - Katashi Tales
Founder - Motivational Strips
Co-President - World Nations Writers Union
Managing Editor - The Genius

# INTRODUCTION

Luzviminda Gabato Rivera is from the Philippines. She is a multi–winning and best-selling author, an excellent international journal reviewer, and a multi-awarded researcher.

She finished her postgraduate courses with academic distinction and academic excellence awards such as the Doctor of Public Administration (her 6th degree). She took up units leading to a Bachelor of Law.

She has published five books, namely: *A Gift*, *A Gift II*, composed of 71 poems and translations of her *A Gift* in 5 series to 23 languages of 17 countries, *Crossroads II*: *A Poets Life Journey* —4th Anthology of Motivational Strips composed of 83 World's Best Poets which became Amazon bestseller, and *A Memoir of Love* – A Quadrilingual ( English, Italian, French and Spanish) in various poetic forms (free verse, haiku, rhyme scheme, sonnet, and tanka) and *Love Spell – A Collection of Sonnets in Asian and European Languages*. All five books became rank one among the best sellers on Amazon.

Her book, *Poets Unify World* – 6th Anthology of Motivational Strips will be published before the year ends. Also, her poems were published in international e-zines and magazines.

She has received multiple recognitions. The latest is for her literary excellence at par with global standards by Motivational Strips and Gujarat Sahitya Academy of India and 50th Independence Day of Nigeria by Inked with Magic. She was also won first place in the Southeast Asian Continent Poetry Award posthumous tribute to the great poet Kairat Duissenov Parman by Hispanumondial Union of Writers and the 93 poets chosen in the Motivational Strips Anthology for Kairat.

She serves as Administrator for the Philippine Office and one of the four approving editors of Bharath Vision website magazine based in India.

Luzviminda Gabato Riviera amazes us with her ability to render with a polished style, extract the essence of the word, and reveal miracles. Her lyrics are enchanting and savant, transforming matter into spirit in continuous consonance with flight, light, and love. The poet belongs to the category of those for whom poetry represents a natural state.

*A Gift III* is a splendid collection of forty poems on the category of love and friendship, pain and loss and hopes, dreams and inspirations. Her *A Gift* poems in five series were translated into 14 languages. This volume of poetry is a lyrical discourse with overwhelmed resonances of the soul of a remarkable poet.

The book is discreet calligraphy of the poet's feelings with a magic lyrical note into spiritual, revealing Luzviminda's poetry's ethereal quality from which run such poignant sentiments. She transmits emotions with her extraordinary ability to plasticize the deep essences into a generous and sensitive poetic language turning every word into real poetry.

The poet can be considered a militant in the service of uplifting principles, of great ideas and noble feelings. She operates with the beautiful instrument of the word that has miraculous power. Luzviminda pleads with pathos in favor of poetry full of content, open to the world, to the tremendous human ideals able to pour over our hearts the beauty of metaphors with which she formulates memorable, incontestable truths masterfully interprets beautiful feelings.

Love for people and life is the spiritual state's perpetual expression that the poet experiences intensely under the empire of love, peace, harmony, fraternity, integrity, dignity, and truth. She belongs to the category of poets of extraordinary grandeur, unique by the high intensity of the lyrical attitude.

The poems' reading reveals her imagistic universe, the infinite horizon, the loneliness generating of charm, the feeling of distance in shades of infinite depths, and the poet's soul experiences astral nostalgia.

The entire volume of poetry *A Gift III* is distinguished by wisdom, greatness, and nobility, thus mirroring the author's spirit's beauty. The aesthetic value of the poems is fabulous and sprinkled with enchanting lyricism.

**Corina Junghiatu**
Administrator and Publication Coordinator of Motivational Strips
Chief Advisor of World Nations Writer's Union

# REVIEWS

Multi-award winner and best seller Luz invites us on a journey to visit her "Gift 3", after her last release of "Love Spell."

Her "Gift 3" treats three alluring themes, "Friendship & Love," "Pain & Loss," "Inspirations, Hopes & Dreams," which all may come across during one's life, at any point in time.

SAUDADE invades the lonely hearts with sadness, as they are separated by the "never-ending seas," "the vastness of the universe," and, thus, every day becomes harder.

The wishes of Luz of "no goodbyes" take her to the chamber of "Pain & Loss" where the "melancholic waves....and "the cold breeze....." "silent tears....." from her sorrowful eyes... render get to be a "lost soul." with no meaning of existence when "love was gone like the wind."  However sad it might seem, "Inspirations, Hopes and Dreams" show their invaluable presence in responsible professionals who risk their lives to overcome the threat that the world is facing. However, this situation remains unless a breakthrough in medicine happens. While waiting for hope, we need to accept the written answer in "heaven's powerful Living God."

**Magie F-V Vijay-Kumar**
Chief Representative for World National Writers Union for SE Africa and Central Asia*
Chief Editor/Director - SIPAY GLOBAL LITERARY JOURNAL* Regional Director of Motivational Strips - SE Africa and Central Asia* National President of UHE, Peru for Seychelles* Ambassador for Humanity and Humanitarian Development for WCHHD -Ghana

A GIFT III by Luzviminda Gabato Rivera is a collection of magnificent and sublime poems. Luzviminda from the Philippines is a multi-talented poet. Her poems are enchanting and captivating. She makes a permanent place in the reader's heart through her poetry. Motivational Strips promoted her as Administrator of the forum, and she is one of the four approving editors of Bharath Vision website magazine based in India.

Dr. Luzviminda interprets the eternal nature of love in her poems with memorable past moments. "I WILL LIVE FOR YOU" is a lovely romantic poem with exquisite imagery. The poem is a classic example of dedication in love:

"You are the wind beneath my wings
when I want to fly and soar high."

Scenes of pain and loss in love are also in the poems of this collection:

"You are so near yet so far
It may be difficult, but the heart chooses
to beat and live for the memories."

When love takes the shape of memories, then there are both kinds of expressions. The deep feelings of love that encompasses various emotions compel a human being to contemplate. In this situation, a human being becomes more mature than before.

While reading the collection, we find that some poems relate to inspirations, hopes, and dreams. These poems explain the importance of life to us. In Gift III, undoubtedly, there are many poems in the collection, which add sparkle to the eyes and calm down tricky puzzles of mind & heart. I believe that readers will indeed like this collection of poems. Luzviminda's poetry will be widely read and appreciated. A Gift III  is another beautiful gift for poetry lovers and readers, after A Gift & A Gift ll. I wish the author many congratulations and continued success.

**Dr. Shailesh Gupta Veer**
(Poet & Reviewer)
Fatehpur, UP, India

I have been privileged to read the excellent book, A Gift III by Luzviminda Gabato Rivera, a very accomplished writer and poet that will take you on a beautiful journey of her unique and talented mind, a must for all poetry lovers. She can keep you transfixed in her words and paints an everlasting picture in the readers' minds. Bravo! Cheers to a poet for another great book to adorn the shelves of the avid poetry reader.


**William T Fearby**
Poet and Founder of Poems of Life


"Life is so generous a giver. But we, judging its gifts by their wrappings, throw them away by our ignorance. Remove the wraps, and you will find beneath it a living splendor, woven of love by wisdom, with power."

Through her love-filled eyes, our friend Luzviminda discovered the gifts of Life and undid the wraps of ego, and found their true splendor. Her latest book of poems, GIFT III is ample testimony to the truth of the quote by Fra Giovanni, an Italian writer. Luzviminda has found the very meaning of Life by finding out the gifts of Life. It's also a purpose by giving them out to us in the form of a book containing beautiful verses.

Like a constellation in which perception and purpose are stars, GIFT III is fantastic poetic work. Marrying poetry with purpose, Luzviminda's GIFT III launches us to a phenomenal poetic trip that loops through time, following love and friendship, and searching for meaning. Luzviminda's writings are heartwarming, charming, and filled with the joys of friendship and love.

GIFT III really would make the most beautiful gift to celebrate the wonder of love and friendship. GIFT III is divided into three categories on LOVE AND FRIENDSHIP, PAIN AND LOSS and INSPIRATION, HOPE AND DREAMS. Poems in this book are in five series and have been translated into forty languages worldwide. I am sure this book will be one of the international bestsellers.

## K. Radhakrishnan
Author of *REFLECTION OF MY SOUL, ERUPTION OF BOTTLED UP EMOTIONS, MOODS IN MOTION* and DAZZLING *DANCE OF POESY*

Luz Rivera demonstrates a deep connection with the senses. Her poetry speaks to the feelings of comfort, peacefulness, happiness, refreshing the stresses of life. Take a stroll with this poet by the brookside, feeling the misty water sprinkling your face, appreciates the simplicities of life. Perhaps your heart will warm from memories of your loves. Tears may stream down your face from memories of those who are no longer at your touch. You will experience these things and more with the beautiful alliterations of Luz Rivera's poetic expressions.

## Liza Joy Tomey
Editor-Fine Lines Literary Journal
The Prolific P

If I opined the intrinsic nature of Gift, I would say we need to start wearing new lenses to be able to comprehend the holistic essence of any Gift, not in terms of its monetary value, rather by imbibing its innate fragrance and allowing its munificent lusciousness to permeate into us.

Through Gift 3, the author, Mrs. Rivera, who is lauded for her refreshing, distinct poetry weaving styles, takes the readers on an enchanting, perspective-molding literary- carousel ride. Even a mere cursory glance into the eclectic plethora that Gift 3 depicts, classified into three mesmerizing categories, will certainly tug you deeper into its captivating, metaphorical values. I fervently recommend this book to each poetry lover who is keen to wear some alluring poetry cardigans and views poetry as a soul transcending experience.

## Jyoti Nair

Capability Development Manager– Talent Transformation and Centre Of Excellence, with a leading global IT solutions, consulting and business solutions organization.
Contributing poet at Delhi Post- DP, a digital media start up published by Institute of Poverty and Governance- IPG, an independent non-profit organization based in New Delhi.

# PRELUDE

# TO

# LOVE

# Amore Mio

Accept me as I am, with my imperfections
And see my weaknesses as my strength.

Drown me with your affection
that is deeper than the deepest sea

Excite me with your kindness
uncountable as the stars in the cosmos.

Thrill me with your overflowing patience
that keeps no record of my wrongdoings

Mesmerize me with your surprises
till the eyes shed tears of happiness.

Embrace me till I couldn't breath
and bring me into paradise.

all of it -------

Love me….

unconditional…

boundless…

endless…

Till the Last Breath of your soul...

# ALBANIAN TRANSLATION
By Sherife Allko

## Amore Mio

Më prano ashtu siç jam, me papërsosmëritë e mia
Dhe shiko dobësitë e mia si forcën time.
Më mbyt me afeksionin tënd
që është më e thellë se deti më i thellë
Më eksitoni me mirësinë tuaj
të panumërueshëm si yjet në kozmos.
Më emocciononi me durimin tuaj të tejmbushur
që nuk mban shënime për keqbërjet e mia
Më hipnotizoni me të papriturat tuaja
derisa sytë të derdhin lot lumturie.
Më përqafoni derisa nuk munda të marr frymë
dhe më sillni në parajsë.

të gjithë atë -------
Më duaj….
pa kushte
e pakufishme
pafund
Deri në Frymën e Fundit të shpirtit tuaj …

# ASSAMESE TRANSLATION
## Malakshmi Borthakur

# মোৰ প্রিয়তম

মূল ইংৰাজী – লুজৱিমিণা গাবেট' ৰিৱেৰা
অসমীয়া অনুবাদ – মালঞ্চী বৰঠাকুৰ


মোক গ্রহণ কৰা, মোৰ অপূর্ণতাখিনিৰ সেতে
আৰু মোৰ অক্ষমতাখিনিক মোৰ সামর্থ হিচাপে
লোৱা !
ডুবি যাবলৈ দিয়া মোক তোমাৰ মৰমৰ গভীৰতাত,
যি মৰম সুগভীৰ সাগৰতকৈও গভীৰ !
মোক সক্রিয় কৰি তোলা তোমাৰ দয়াশীলতাৰে,
যি এই ব্রহ্মাণ্ডও জুৰি ব্যাপ্ত তৰাৱলীৰ দৰেই অগণনীয়
!
মোক ৰোমাঞ্চিত কৰি তোলা তোমাৰ অপৰিসীম
ধৈর্যৰ দ্বাৰা,
যি কেতিয়াও মই কৰা অপৰাধবিলাকৰ লিখিত
টোকা নাৰাখে !
মোক মন্ত্রমুগ্ধ কৰি তোলা তোমাৰ আশ্চর্যৰে,
যেতিয়ালৈকে মোৰ দুচকুৰে সুখৰ চকুলো নিগৰি নাহে
!

মোক সাৱতি ধৰা এনেকৈ যাতে মোৰ উশাহ বন্ধ হৈ
যায়,
আৰু মোক স্বৰ্গীয় সুখৰ অনুভূতি দিয়া !

মই বিচাৰোঁ এই সকলোখিনি তোমাৰ পৰা...
মোক প্ৰেম দিয়া ...!
যি নিঃচৰ্ত ...!
যি অপৰিসীম ...  !
যি অনন্ত ...  !
তোমাৰ   শেষ নিশ্বাসলৈকে ...  !

# BENGALI TRANSLATION
Queen Sarkar

# আমার ভালোবাসা

আমার যেমন অসম্পূর্ণতা রয়েছে তেমনি আমাকেও গ্রহণ
করো
এবং আমার দুর্বলতাগুলিকে আমার শক্তি হিসাবে দেখো।
তোমার ভালোবাসায়
গভীরতম সমুদ্রের চেয়ে গভীর এ আমাকে নিয়ে চলো
ব্রম্মাণ্ডর অগণিত তারা দের মত
তোমার উদারতায় আমায় উত্তেজিত করে।
তোমার উপচে পড়া ধৈর্য দিয়ে আমাকে শিহরিত করো
যা আমার অন্যায়ের কোনো প্রমাণ না রাখে
তোমার বিস্ময়ে আমাকে মন্ত্রমুগ্ধ করো
যতক্ষণ না আমার চোখ সুখের অশ্রু তে ভরে
আমি নিঃশ্বাস ত্যাগ না করা পর্যন্ত আমাকে জড়িয়ে ধরো
এবং আমাকে সর্গে নিয়ে এসো।
পুরোপুরি

# BRAZILIAN TRANSLATION
## Shakil Kalam

## Meu Amor

Aceite-me como eu sou, com minhas imperfeições
E veja minhas fraquezas como minha força.
Me afogue com seu carinho
isso é mais profundo do que o mar mais profundo
Me excite com sua gentileza
incontáveis como as estrelas do cosmos.
Me emocione com sua paciência transbordante
que não mantém nenhum registro de meus erros
Me hipnotize com suas surpresas
até os olhos derramarem lágrimas de felicidade.
Abrace-me até eu não conseguir respirar
e me traga para o paraíso.
tudo isso -------
Me ame….
incondicional…
sem limites ...
infinito ...
Até o último suspiro de sua alma...

# DARI TRANSLATION
## Parwez Hashimi


تحفه ششم:_


با عیوب خود مرا مرا مرا بپذیر و نقاط ضعف خود را به عنوان قدرت من ببین. مرا با محبت خود غرق کن که عمیق تر مرا با مهربانی تو غیرقابل          از عمیق ترین دریا است تحمل ستارگان کیهان را تحریک کن. مرا با صبر و شکیبایی پرت کنید.

که هیچ سابقه ای از اعمال ناگوار من ندارد ، مرا با تعجب خود شگفت زده کرد تا اینکه چشمان اشک شادی مرا در آغوش بگیرید تا من نتوانم نفس بکشم و مرا به. ریخت بهشت برسانم. همه آن ------- من را دوست دارم ...

بی قید و شرط... بی حد و حصر... بی پایان... تا آخرین نفس روح شما...

# GUJARATI TRANSLATION
## Bhanubhai Patel

# પ્રેમમારો પ્રેમ

મારી અપૂર્ણતાની સાથે જેમ હું છું તેમ મને સ્વીકાર
અને મારી નબળાઇઓને મારી શક્તિ તરીકે જો .

મને તારાં સ્નેહમાં ડૂબાડ
જે સૌથી ઊંડા સમુદ્ર કરતાં ઊંડો છે

તારી કૃપાથી મને ઉત્તેજિત કર
બ્રહ્માંડ માં તારાઓની જેમ અસંખ્ય.

તારાં ઉભરાઈ રહેલા ધૈર્યથી મને રોમાંચિત કર
જે મારા ખોટા કર્મોનો કોઈ રેકોર્ડ રાખતો નથી

તારા આશ્ચર્ય વડે મને સંમોહિત કર
જ્યાં સુધી મારી આંખો ખુશીના આંસુઓ ના વહાવે.

હું શ્વાસ ન લઈ શકું ત્યાં સુધી મને ભેટ
અને મને સ્વર્ગમાં લાવ.

તે બધા -

મને પ્રેમ કર....

બિનશરતી...

અનહદ...

અનંત...

# PASHTO TRANSLATION
Parwez Hashimi

## شبرومه دالی

ما ومنه زما له نقص سره،او زما د ضعف نقطي زما قوت وګنه،ما د خپلي ميني پواسطه غرقه کړه چی له زور سپند څخه ژوره ده.
ما پخپلي مهربانۍ سره وهڅوه.
دکهکشان د غیرقابل شمار ستورو ، ماته په صبر کولو طاقت راکړه چی زما د غلطیو هیڅ اثر به نه ثبتیږي.
ما غافیلګیره کړه،تر څو له سترګو می د خوشحالۍ اوبنکي وبهیږي،ما په غیږ کی ونیسه تر څو ونشم کولی ساه واخله او ما جنت ته ورسوه.
له ټولو_ما سره مینه وکړه.

# PUNJABI TRANSLATION
Mohit Katyal

)

# ਮੇਰੇ ਇਸ਼ਕ

ਮੈਨੂੰ ਮੇਰੀ ਕਮੀਆਂ ਦੇ ਨਾਲ ਅਪਨਾ ਲੈ
ਅਤੇ ਮੇਰੀ ਕਮਜ਼ੋਰੀਆਂ ਨੂੰ ਤਾਕਤ ਬਨਾ ਲੈ

ਮੈਨੂੰ ਆਪਣੇ ਪਿਆਰ ਵਿੱਚ ਡੁੱਬਾ ਲੈ
ਇਹ ਸਭ ਤੋਂ ਡੂੰਘੇ ਸਮੁੰਦਰ ਨਾਲੋਂ ਡੂੰਘਾ ਹੈ

ਮੈਨੂੰ ਆਪਣੀ ਦਿਆਲਤਾ ਨਾਲ ਸਾਭੰ ਲੈ
ਇਸ਼ਕ ਬ੍ਰਹਿਮੰਡ ਦੇ ਤਾਰਿਆਂ ਵਾਂਗ ਅਣਗਿਣਤ ਹੈ.

ਆਪਣੇ ਸਬਰ ਨਾਲ ਮੈਨੂੰ ਰੋਮਾਂਚਿਤ ਕਰਦੇ
ਉਹ ਮੇਰੀਆਂ ਗਲਤੀਆਂ ਦਾ ਕੋਈ ਹਿਸਾਬ ਨਹੀਂ ਰੱਖਦਾ

ਮੈਨੂੰ ਆਪਣੇ ਹੈਰਾਨੀ ਨਾਲ ਯਾਦ ਕਰ
ਜਦੋਂ ਤੱਕ ਮੇਰੀਆਂ ਅੱਖਾਂ ਖੁਸ਼ੀ ਦੇ ਹੰਝੂ ਵਹਾਉਣ ਨਹੀਂ ਦਿੰਦੀਆਂ.

ਮੈਨੂੰ ਗਲੇ ਲਗਾ ਜਦ ਤਕ ਮੈਂ ਸਾਹ ਨਹੀਂ ਲੈ ਸਕਾ
ਅਤੇ ਮੈਨੂੰ ਫਿਰਦੌਸ ਵਿੱਚ ਲੈ ਆ

# SETSWANA TRANSLATION
Kenneth Maswabi

## Lorato lele makatsang

Nkamogela jaaka kentse, le tsotlhe tse disenyegileng
O bone bokowa jwame ele bokgone
Nkhurumetsa ka lorato lwa gago
Le boteng jwa lone bo fetang jwa lowatle
Intumedise ka bosiame jwa gago
Gago kgonwe go bala boteng jwa gago jaaka dinaledi
mo loaping
Mphe boitumelo ka iketlo ya pelo ya gago
Pelo ee sa beeng sepe sese bosula
Nkgogomose maikutlo ka tse o difitlhileng
Go fitlhela matlho a me a kopakopetsa dikeledi
Nkatumela o atle go fitlhela mowa wame o tsamaya
O ntseye o nkise mo boiketlong jwa legodimo
Gotlhe gotlhe
O nthate
Go sena lobaka
Go feteletse
Go sena bokhutlo
Go fitlhelela mowa wa gago wa bofelo o tsamaya

# TAMIL TRANSLATION
Radhakrishan Krishnan

என்னுடைய குறைவுகளோடு என்னை
ஏற்றுக்கொள் .


என்னுடைய பலகீனத்தையும்
வலிமையாக கண்டுகொள்


கடல் போன்ற ஆழமுடைந்த உன்
பாசத்தில் என்னை முழுக செய்


வானத்தில்  உள்ள எண்ணமுடியாத
நட்ஷத்திரங்கள் போல் அளவிலாத
கருணை மூலம் என்னை உவகை
அடையச்செய்


என்னுடைய தவறுகளுக்கு கணக்கு
வைத்துக்கொள்ளாமல் உன் பொங்கும்

பொறுமையினால் என்னை மகிழ்ச்சி அடைய செய்

என் கண்களில் இருந்து ஆனந்த கண்ணீர் வரும் வரை வியப்படைய வைத்து என்னை மயக்கு .

நான் மூச்சுக்கு திண்டாடும் வரையில் என்னை அணைத்து எனக்கு பேரின்பம் கொடு .

எல்லையில்லாத ,

அளவில்லாத ,

முடிவில்லாத

அன்புடன் உன் ஸ்வாசத்தின் முடிவுவரை காதலினால் மகிழ செய்

# TELUGO TRANSLATION
Rama Krishna Perugo

# అమోర్ మియో

నా లోపాలతో, నన్ను నేనున్నట్లుగా అంగీకరించండి

మరియు నా బలహీనతలను నా బలంగా చూడండి.

నీ ఆప్యాయతతో నన్ను ముంచివేసింది

అది లోతైన సముద్రం కంటే లోతుగా ఉంటుంది

నీ దయతో నన్ను ఉత్తేజపరచండి

విశ్వంలో ఉన్న నక్షత్రాల వలె లెక్కించలేనిది.

మీ పొంగిపొర్లుతున్న సహనంతో నన్ను థ్రిల్ చేయండి

అది నా తప్పుల గురించి రికార్డ్ చేయదు

మీ ఆశ్చర్యాలతో నన్ను మంత్రముగ్ధులను చేయండి

నా కళ్ళు ఆనందం కన్నీళ్లు పెట్టుకునే వరకు.

నేను ఊపిరి తీసుకోని వరకు నన్ను ఆలింగనం చేసుకోండి

నన్ను స్వర్గానికి తీసుకురండి.

ఇవన్నీ -

నన్ను ప్రేమించు….

టేషరతుగా…

అనంతమైన…

అంతులేని…

మీ ఆత్మ యొక్క చివరి శ్వాస వరకు …!

# VIETNAMESE TRANSLATION
## HONG NGOC CHAU

# TÌNH YÊU CỦA TÔI

Hãy chấp nhận tôi như đã nói
Tuy không hoàn hảo nhưng là tôi
Và xem điểm yếu là không yếu
Điểm mạnh của tôi sẽ hiện thôi

Nhấn đuối tôi bằng tình cảm bạn
Thật sâu đáy biển nơi sâu hơn
Làm tôi phấn khích với lòng tốt
Vô số như sao trên quảng không

Kiên nhẫn bạn làm tôi xúc động
Không lưu tâm những viêc làm sai
Khiến tôi mê hoặc tôi kinh ngạc
Hạnh phúc bất ngờ nước mắt rơi.

Ôm nhé đến khi tôi hết thở
Và đưa tôi đến cõi thiên đường.
Hãy yêu tôi nhé không điều kiện
Hồn thở cuối cùng mãi vấn vương

# ON

# FRIENDSHIP

# AND

# LOVE

# Because of Your Love !

Because of your love…
I see life in different perspectives
Soar on greater heights
Despite the robust wind
I await the rainbows after the storm
To be resilient during endless struggles
When life seemed in grey scale
Flickering lights brightens my path
-above all-
When everything has fallen
Your love always lifts me up
Oh! I can't imagine life without you
Because of your love…
Life on earth has become a paradise

# Drifted Into Paradise

Amid the night

As the moon reigns in the sky

And light surrenders to darkness

Rises the silhouette of a mortal

As he slowly approaches his goddess

She vividly sees his countenance

His looks invigorate her soul

Faltering her pulses when he talks

A soul of few words

Spilling an ocean of witticism

As the stillness of the night

Hypnotizes their souls

Savoring the essence of their existence

They lay entwined in each other's arms

And their souls surrender to

The spell of love

Till they drift into paradise.

# How did I fall in Love?

How did I fall in love?

To you my dear friend

Everything is unplanned

It is the fate's will

That our paths crossed

Be a part of each other's journey

Every time I see you

My loves go yonder

I begin to love all of you

My heart never stops beating

When I talk to you

I am out of words

And I start to tremble

I do not want to say goodbye

I do not want to be alone

I want to stay with you

For the rest of my life.

# I Will Live For You

You are the air I breathe

The sun that gives light when darkness creeps into
my innermost being .

You are stars that continue to blink despite my
imperfections

… that wipe away the tears
from the hurdles of life.

You are the wind beneath my wings
when I want to fly and soar high.

The rainbow that gives colors to my life
when hope is no longer to be found.

You are the waves that never stop kissing the
seashore to show your endless love for me

-Above all -
When everything is gone
I Promise, My king


I will continue to live
Because
You are the greatest reason for my living.

# Joy To My Heart

Sweet humming of the birds
Rustling of the leaves
Whistling of the winds
Resultant exquisite sound of waves
-All of it-
A lovely lullaby
A pleasant to the ears
Invigorates the soul
Like your presence
A joy to my heart

# Love In Multitask

In the midst of unforetold journey
When everything was panicky
You came into my life honey
And made it taste like winey.


Once upon a time in my lowlife
Everything I beheld was full of strife
It changed in a glance and made it rife
Your presence is a joy to my life


Fate has done an awesome task
Crossing our paths in a flask
In times when everyone is in face mask
I never thought love is in multitask.

# None Like You...

You make the sun shines
and gives light to my gloomy life .

You make the stars glitter at night
and make me shine my brightest.

You always make the rainbows appear
After the storms and give life to my dying hope.

You are the wind beneath my wings
That makes me soar on greater heights.

You gathered the pieces and turned me into whole
The missing piece I'd longed to see.

Your presence is the most wonderful gift
this life has ever received.

That keeps my heart beating and
Make me live once again....

# Promise! You Will Hold Me In Your Life

Promise! You will hold me in your life

Our hopes and dreams

The blunder we fought

The caring and love

Wonderful moments

Memories of a lifetime.


Promise! You will hold me in your life

The love I give you

Even winds may change

Everything has fallen

My heart only beats for you

Till the last breath of my soul….

# Querencia

The view of sparkling lights

countless accolades flaunt

endless clash of wit and

deafening sounds of triumph

cosmos that is the soul's pirouette

she creeps silently, hidden

to the eyes of restless souls

Into your memories that continue to

pulsate the blood vessels of her heart

a haven for the soul, a gift

A querencia that she always dreamt.

**QUERENCIA - a place where one's strength is drawn, where one feels at home, the place where are your most authentic self

# Saudade

From a distance

Million miles away

Across never ending seas

Distant and tall mountains

Unconquerable vastness of the universe

All Between us

Makes every day harder

The yearning to be near each day

To be held in your arms and console my heart

To feel your endless love

My life's missing piece

Now my life is full of wishes

If wishes can come true ......

The wish that day would come

I wish that mystical fate will be our side

And our love will see us through

To the journey of no goodbyes.


Saudade – the love that remains a desire to be near
someone or something distant

# Serendipity

Meeting you by serendipity
Makes my life full of gaiety
Moments with you stir me in glee
In my heart, love finds it way.

You are the missing piece
I'd long to see
In your presence, Life is easy
I am lost when you walk away.

I've never been so happy
In this life that is full of misery
Thoughts of you brighten my day
Never leave again and make me lonely.

I promise as long as I am breathing free
My heart will keep on beating for thee
You are the reasons for my existence
With you my life will be full of essence.

# The Heart Will Never forget

To a dear friend...

Your benevolent heart

a solace to my soul

I will hold dearly in life

I will always write the story

of friendship and love

memories of fun and laughter

As you are embarking on a  new journey

I wish you peace and happiness

this world can offer

When I am lost and gone in the wind

I promise to hold you in my life

For there are no goodbyes .....

As I cherish and walk beyond life

I promise ......

The heart will never forget.

# Tonight the moon laughs...

Every night it ascended in the cosmos

Giving light to the dimness of the night

Wandering in the vastness of nowhere

Buried in seclusion during the day

For years, life has forgotten

Lights slowly fading into view

Before oblivion envelopes its nothingness

Mesmerizing and spectacular rays

from the Star were sighted

Sparkling like a diamond .....

The moon suddenly winks its eyes

and purses it lips

A wonderful smile that vibrates to its heart

Tonight, the moon laughs and ascends

With the stars that once joined its journey

every night and day.....

Forever and beyond......

# To You I Promise

Knowing you is the best thing

That ever happens in my life

You give meaning in it

That once lost and forgotten

Life maybe tough at times

Fate will not be kind

Our roads will be rough

And forever will be hostile

To You I Promise

To treasure our love

To hold you in my heart dearly

And keep it in my soul

Forever and always….

# You Are My Everything

You are my life

My everything

I shall not faint

The remaining days of life

I will give to you

The heart and soul

I pledge so true

Each moment with you

I will cherish

I will always cling to love

And walk on life with you

Till this life is through

# On

# Pain

# And

# Loss

# A Day Without You...

A Day Without You…
Is like a sun that refuses to shine
Lonesome clouds that stop wandering
Brilliant and fleeting rainbow has dimmed and pale
Soothing wind increasingly frigid
Wave that failed to kiss the seashore
Glorious moon became melancholic and
the night seemed so endless.
A dream that turned into a nightmare
A paradise that became an abbey
-All of it-
I cannot stand life ..
Because A day without you....
Means dying a million times....

# Beginning To Its End

Horizon has become deemed

Sun has failed to shine

Wind stings like a bee

Wonderful mornings

became a deafening silence

Beautiful nights have lost their essence

Sweet nothings slowly acclimated to

Its natural death

Thoughtfulness became

A dreaded disease

Everything is welcoming

the beginning to its end.

# Butterfly and Its Broken Wings

The Kaleidoscope display of flora has turned
into grey scale
The beautiful flowers that dance have become
apathetic
The sunshine that illuminates the vastness of
atmosphere has dimmed
Chirping crickets half-way reaching their
crescendo
The cold breeze stings like a bee
A paradise that became an abbey to the
mourning soul of the fragile, golden-winged
butterfly
Unable to fly and conquer greater heights
And the desire to traverse life has vanished

# Broken

The deafening sounds of the waves
kisses the seashore
cold breeze envelopes her nothingness
fine sand tickles her feet
slowly her hands scoop the fine sand
toss it in the air, as she watches the
the sun hides in the cosmos
bringing melancholic thoughts
to her mind and pain in her heart
swiftly life's strife is rekindling in the sky
a walk down memory lane
like a dagger that breaks her heart
and vibrates to her dying soul
silent tears are rolling down in her cheeks
the lone witness to her never - ending anguish
To love …..
lost……
shattered……

# Elusive Fate

As the sun bid goodbye

Dark and coppery clouds

Listlessly wondering in the sky

And melancholic waves continue

Kissing the seashore.


While the cold breeze

envelopes her nothingness

Silent tears borne from

her sorrowful eyes

stems from the broken hearts

and lost soul.

Her hopes vanished when
Love was gone like the wind
Faded away the reasons
for existence

If Love will lead him back
Only the elusive fate knows

Someday….

# Far Away

Her eyes are staring at nothingness

tears are battling her last strength

weakness creeps to her nerves

mind drifts into oblivion

far away from pains that are

perennially stubbing the core of her soul

that serves death a million times.

# If I Ask You

If I ask you
Would your heart and mind consider?

The silent tears
wiped away by your love and affection

The brokenness of life
fixed by the rainbows in the horizon

The momentous nights and beautiful mornings
give life to my dying soul

The longing for a beautiful soul
To spend the remaining days of my life

The promises of love ...
boundless.. endless..
Till the last breath of my soul…

# Reaching Out

Since you've been gone
Life's not been easy
You bring with you
My heart and soul
Forgetting you is impossible
You had given me
So much to remember
Away from you
Is like a sail without direction
A journey without the ending
A life without  meaning
Please come back
End this misery I am feeling
I am reaching out
I hope you feel it
Let my mornings
be filled with sunshine
And my nights with excitement
Restore the life that was lost

Please comeback
Hear my cry, Oh! Loud..
Bring back the "ullassa"
that turned to blue
I am reaching out…
Please come back…

# Spirits Lament

On the steep hill lies a beautiful house
A witness of endless love borne from souls
Princess happily living with her spouse
"Till death do us part" was their mutual goals.

One day, the house was covered with darkness
Laughter had turned to deafening outcry
Splashes of blood, mirror of awfulness
From dagger, two souls surrendered and died.

Every night, moaning of souls could be heard
Pleading for life and endless agony
Their appearances in white clothes were conferred
People near the hill bore testimony.

Spirits kept on lamenting on the hill
Asking for justice nobody could fill

# Tonight Her Tears fall



The dimness of the night

creeps to her innermost soul

As her mind succumbs to tiredness

from today's toil

Slowly, she closes her eyes

to feel the silence of the night

while the cold breeze

envelopes her nothingness

she feels the streaming tears

running down her face

drowning her bleeding heart

with deep anguish and

not even a million turquoise rings

could console her.

# Verses of Life

Into thy hands, brilliant ink flowed,
A Poetic pillar that came into this world.
Blessed by the living Creator above
With a heart so gracious and filled with love.

As you walked into the verses of life
Unfathomable love for literature did arise
You've set your pace nor could you cease
To support the literature and peace.

Your noble heart had touched all poets
You inspired us all with your lovely sonnets.
Selflessly uplifting each intellectual soul
Leaving a splendid legacy for humanity in bold.

As your journey continues to reap glory
For the world literature and humanity
You taught us the meaning of humility
As we venture into the world of poetry.

You left a mark on this world with your imprints.
From your vision and legacy literature profits.
Love for literature is what you imparted.
Never to be forgotten now you're departed.

# When Goodbye is not Forever

The sun slowly surrenders to the dimness of the
night

As the moon traverses the vastness
of cosmos

The cold breeze soothes her innermost being

While the chirping crickets bring her to senses.

Silent tears are clouding the windows to her soul

As the memories of yesterday spring to her mind

The unmeasurable gaiety that is hard to contain

The promises of beautiful mornings that bring
excitement

The inspiration to conquer greater heights

The strength to hurdle the ambiguities of life

It's been years and my heart is still in deep anguish

It died when you left and still dying a million times

Unable to grasp the reasons of your leaving

You are so near yet so far

It may be difficult but the heart chooses

to beat and live for the memories

Hoping that someday love will lead you back

and then you will stay.

# ON

# INSPIRATIONS

# HOPES

# AND

# DREAMS

# Beautiful India

India is a beautiful country to behold
An economy like a growing tiger ever bold
With an impressive line-up of languages told
Religious beliefs and practices they always uphold

A megadiverse country of the world
Wildlife sanctuaries were done as a stronghold
Biosphere reserves are millionfold
Animals and plants are treated like gold.

Such mesmerizing art and architecture
Taj Mahal is India's outstanding structure
Tradition, styles. music, and a mixed culture
Family values are looked at as superstructure

India's literature, I've come to know better
Indian poets make the world better
Each seeking the well-being of humanity as a gifted
writer
Irrespective of color, race, and culture

Oh! How I long to visit and see your lands
Beautiful India and the motherland
Where everybody loves being in a pastureland
Promising a beautiful tomorrow for everyone

# Beyond My Limits

I never knew life has more to offer
Until you came into my life
You saw in me that I've never seen before
And pushed me beyond my limits.

You stir in me that life is a continuous journey
Complacency should never be embraced
Being competent and competitive
Is what I should desire.

You have inspired me so much
To conquer the greater heights
Spread my wings and never falter
Success can never be far behind.

As I walk on life and see the milestone
Success I am reaping beyond measure
On this day and always, I show my gratitude
Pushing me beyond limits, I am forever grateful

# For How Long

It has been months

The world is under your threat

Greatest scientists and researchers

Were challenged by your existence

Medical doctors, nurses and other health

practitioners continue to risk their lives

Police enforcers and other peacekeepers

were tapped to prevent chaos ------

Many lives succumb to your

Merciless killings


For how long?


The world will be in fear and panic

People will be wearing mask

Social distancing the new protocol

Children are forced to stay at home

Everybody are forced to vow

To the "new normal"

For How long?

This life of uncertainty
Will harbor our mind and hearts
Creating hopelessness and futility
That is hard to subdue…

For how long?

A breakthrough in medicine
Will be discovered
To stop the virus
Destroying the humanity

For how long?

Nobody could give an answer
Not even the brilliant creation
Powerful countries couldn't stop the virus

For How long?


Everything will be normal again.

The answer is written

In the heaven's powerful Living God.

# Hear Our Prayers

It awakens us from deep slumber

Raging rain is frightening to our innermost being
Hostile whistling of the winds is cracking our nerves
Horrifying sounds that are crushing our souls.

Oh! Powerful Living God
We pray for your mercy
And calmness of our souls.

You are the God of everything
Let the typhoon succumb to your power
Finds its way to where it belongs,

We pray for the strength
That will help make us through
And everything will come to pass.

We pray for the everlasting hope
That only comes from you Lord
When everything seems so futile.

Our Lord, we can't wait to see
The rainbow piercing the thunderclouds
When everything is done.

# I Need You...

I need You…
Every minute of my life….
When storms are endless
I seek your warm embrace.
To keep me still
When darkness creeps into my innermost being
I search for the light that soothes my heart and soul.
When I am drowning with what this world can offer
– fame, power, and money
You always made your presence felt, and nothing
else counts in the end.
When hopes are nowhere to be found
I cling to your promises of everlasting life.
When I am lost, and everything has fallen
You always lift me, and I find myself in your loving
arms.
Your unconditional love keeps my heart beating and
inspires me to make my presence in this life count.

# In Everything

It strikes us in our serene state
With global magnitude
While its cause is still unknown
Panic and fear are felt all around
Creating chaos and health threat.

As the world is engaged
It is our part to do our share
Let us put our hands in prayer
As this will come to pass
In God's perfect time.

Let this come to our mind
That in everything there is reason
Gone were the days of nature's destruction
Love for power and wealth
Will be gone in a wink of an eye.

Let this be a realization for us
That nothing belongs to us
Let go of greediness and
earthly things

As everything will perish.
Above all ----

Let us be still and at peace
Put our trust and faith
To the Living God
Our Only Hope
Till the end of time
In His Name.

# Life's Essence

The shatteringly brilliant sun

That gives energy to life

whispering blue ethereal sky

brings everlasting hope and

the vastness of flora excites her eyes

As zephyr embraces her innermost being

She sits down slowly beside

the beautiful flowing brook

Her eyes are twinkling with happiness

As she scoops the cold water and

Let it toss in the air

Swiftly, silent tears are falling

down in her cheeks

The kind of life she always wanted

is unfolding in her eyes

Where she finds peace and happiness

Away from pressures of life and

The brilliance of fame and power

Where she can be at herself

knowing the simplicities of life

Where she finds contentment--

The true essence of life.

# Metanoia

The darkness swiftly creeps
cosmos is silenced by the dying sun
as listless moon tips his hat
to the dimness of night
mirroring the soul's journey
petrified of towering heights
far than eyes could see
greater than the mind could assert
till the revert of sail
initiated by a powerful soul
ignited the flame in heart and mind
the will to withstand
the endless storms
as the rainbow awaits
and blue ethereal sky waves
the welcoming of a new dawn of life
A new beginning
A journey of Metanoia

***Metanoia – The Journey of changing one's mind,

heart, self, or way of life.

# Only You And Me....

Tell Me
How can I be still?

When the world is in chaos
people are slowly dying
to a health threat that is pandemic
Which cause is still unknown.

When countries with enough resources
and technology seem so futile
Brilliant scientists are on double-time
to invent a dose for this unseen threat.

When frontliners are risking their lives
medical doctors, nurses and health care assistants
fearlessly taking care of PUI's and PUM's
without enough Personal Protective Equipment.

When people are in panic
to safeguard for their lives from
the pandemic threat and starvation
With time that is still unknown.

When the governments are
applying measures such as
locked down and social distancing but
people don't seem to care.

When everything is uncertain

and what tomorrow is ahead of us
Nobody can give assurance and
It seems hope is slowly fading.

A voice from afar
Answered me:

My Child…

In everything there is a reason
The beautiful world I've once created
With its purpose to serve your God
Is now tainted with the love of power and
greediness.

The battle of "who's more powerful"
in terms of resources, technology and weapons
is a never-ending quest for power and
My creations are the losers in the end.

When people tend to depend
on their capabilities and
rely more on their material wealth and
forgot the reasons for their existence.

My Child…

Let it be known…
that Human Beings are created with
limitations and imperfections
to realize Living God's power.

the COVID- 19 scenario is an awakening
that there is no one or nothing
You could hold unto…
during the darkest hours..

even …
Power…
Wealth…
Fame…

My Child…
Always remember
In the end….
It is between

ONLY…

YOU and ME….

# ACROSTIC ON METAPHOR

M-esmerizes us from afar with splendor

E- xuding brilliance, yet nursing own pain

T- ruly she bears a burden so great

A--ppreciation is her only antidote to
worry

P–ure and reverential thanks giving
irrespective

H- er light may grow deem but not her
generous heart

O-nly with helping others she finds true
fulfilment

R-eflecting inner peace, as her love conquers
own weakness.

# When the Seagulls Fly

Ever restless seagulls conquering the vastness
of horizon
Uncurtailed independence to soar on greater
heights
Above the drama and emotional boundaries
When times get rough
Fearlessness pulsates in the blood vessels of
the heart
Sparkling optimism vibrates to the soul
Today, I let my seagulls in me flourish
Let my wings soar the unconquerable heights
Steadfast and fearless
Let my heart and soul delve into the ocean of
possibilities
Till the vastness of horizon
Is within my reach

# YOU are my Everything

## I thank Thee everytime……


When I open my eyes every morning
To see Your wonderful creation
When I hear the "lab dab" of my heart
I Know that Your love continues to give me life.


When I started to move my body and my brain
controls the movement of my muscles
I feel how powerful You are
I am amazed how you perfectly placed the organs
and
How they are interdependent with each other.


When I look up in the sky, I see your brilliance
Through those marvelous and wandering clouds
How they process the water and continues to give
life.


I see the radiance of the sun
How they never fail to bring light to the earth every
daylight and manage to revolve around its axis.
I see the moon, stars and planets that were designed
according to the Lord's purpose.
When I experience storms, earthquake and various
calamities, I know your boundless love by helping
me make it through it all.

As I traverse the wonderful journey of life
And encounter the storms
I realize that nobody and no-one
Has loved me and continues loving me despite my
imperfection.

As I continue to embark in this beautiful life
Whatever countless achievements and blessings
That may come my way…
I will continue to thank Thee.

Because without YOU…
I AM NOTHING.

# Your Promises…

It is Your Promises …
That calm my life
It gives peace
to my troubled hearts.

You are my strength
In times of my weaknesses
My shield to the storms of life
When I can no longer fought

You are my refuge
To my restless soul
Your love is boundless
I always hold in my life

Your Promises…
Is the joy to my sorrow
the light to my path
That give me hope

To eternity and beyond..

# A

# GIFT

# IN

# FIVE SERIES

# TRANSLATION

# ON

# PHILIPPINES

# LANGUAGES

# TRANSLATION

# ON

# A

# GIFT 1

# A GIFT

You've inspired me more than anybody else
To strive for more learning and improve my craft
You've shown me how to be competent
And to remain humble despite
countless achievements.

Days will never be the same again
Without your friendship in my life
They called you a star, but I call you a diamond
Who shines brightly by showing other people's
worth.

Days in this lifetime will never be enough
To show my appreciation of a God-given gift
Perfectly wrapped with overflowing talents and
wisdom--
An ullassa that I dreamed of someday.

I know it is too much to request
To please promise me to always be around
No matter how hard it is
No matter what it takes
For I shall dwell and
Walk in our friendship forever

# PANGASINENSE TRANSLATION
By John Flores

## SAY REGALO

Anggapoy arum ya toon angiter na ligliwa ed siak nu
aga sika
Pyan manpeleng ya manaral nin maung san baluen su
say kaksilan ko
Inpanengneng mod siak nu panuntoy manmaliw ya
matunong
San manmaliw ya mapaabeba angganu
agla nabilang su bale balen agamuran.


Say agew anggad kapigan agla manmaliw ya pareho
Nu anggapoy pipiyulop mo ed bilay ko
Tinawag dakan bitewen, pero say tawag kod sika
dyamante
Ya manpapaliwawa ed panagpanengneng na gunguna
daray toon
arum.


Saray agew ed sayan leneg na panbilay anggad
kapigan aga unsustu
Pyan naipanengneng kod sikay panagmaliw kod
regalon inter na Katawan
Inbalkot dan maratdakep ed masayaksak a talento
tan
inkanayari - -

Say liket ya akugip ko panakar ya panaun.


Antak ya masulosulok yan ikerew
Ya panpanangasim ipormisam ed siak ya lanang kan
wadtan
Angganu panuntoy irap tan
Angganu antoy nagawa
Unpirmi ak san
Unakar ed ulupan tan anggad angga.

# TAGALOG TRANSLATION
Zaldy F. Perez

# ANG UNANG REGALO

Ikaw ang naging inspirasyon ng higit kanino man.
Upang magsumikap at pagbutuhin aking talento
Ipinakita mo sa akin kung paano maging karampatang
bilang ako
At manatiling mapagkumbaba sa likod ng di mabilang na
tagumpay.

Ang mga araw ay hindi na magkatulad muli
Kung wala ang iyong pagkakaibigan sa aking buhay palagi
Tinatawag ka nilang isang bituin, sa aki'y isa kang
brilyante
Na nagliliwanag sa pamamagitan ng puhagpapahalaga sa
ibang tao

Araw sa buhay na ito'y hindi magiging sapat
Upang ipakita ang aking pagpapahalaga sa regalong
ibinigay ng Maykapal
Perpektong nakabalot ng umaapaw na talento at
karunungan
Isang " Ulassa" na pinapangarap ko balang araw
Alam kong sobra ang aking hinihiling
Upang mangyari ang isang pangako
Na lagi ka sa aking tabi
Kahit gaano man kahirap ito
Anuman ang mangyari
Sapagkat ako'y tatahan at..
Maglalakbay kasama ang ating pagkakaibigan

# TRANSLATION

# ON

# A

# GIFT 1I

# A GIFT II

The sky is bright and gay
Night is bejeweled with enchanting stars with
the moon and its beautifully crafted trenches

From afar, the chirping crickets are pleasing to the
ears
Creating a loquacious night till the break of dawn.
Come, the beautiful night is pleading
Let us drink the water that
Runs to the rivers that mend
broken hearts and souls.
Oh, let us endure to treasure
a Gift that seems to disappear but is
still breathing and continuing to
give life to the broken hopes and dreams
Bridle the lost course and
find meaning to lost soul.
Oh! Let us endure to treasure a Gift
Come the beautiful night is pleading.

# PANGASINENSE TRANSLATION
By John Flores

# SAY REGALON KUMADWA

Say tawen maliwawa tan magayaga
Labi akawesan na mankidyam ya bitewen kaibay
Bulan tan say marakep a ginawan dalan

Manlapud arawi, say kansyon na kuliglig marakep
dengelen ed layag
Mangaggaway maingal ya labi anggad palbangon.
Galila, mikakasi su marakep ya labi
Uninom tayoy danum ya
Unaagos ed ilog ya mangaapiger na
Puso tan kipapasen asakitan
O, mantepel tayu pyan mansilbi
Say regalo ya singa naaandi balet
Siyansya nin uniingas san untutuloy pyan
mangiter bilay ed saray  aderal a ilalo tan pangarap
Tundaan su abalang a imanu tan
anapen ed abalang a kipapasen.
O! itepel tayu pyan mansilbi su regalo
Gilala say marakep ya labi mikakasi.

# TAGALOG TRANSLATION
## Zaldy F. Perez


## ANG PANGALAWANG REGALO


Ang langit ay maliwanag at masaya
Ang gabi ay hiyas na may kaakit-akit na mga bituin
Kasama ang buwan at ang kanyang magagandang gawa
Mula sa malayo, ang mga huni ng kamaro ay nakalulugod
sa mga tainga
Sa paglikha ng isang maliwanag na gabi hanggang sa
madaling araw
Uminom tayo ng tubig sa ilog na
Kayang umayos ng mga puso at damdaming wasak
O, tiisin natin ang sakit at pahalagahan
Isang regalo na tila nawawala
Ngunit patuloy na nagbibigay buhay
Sa mga nasirang pag-asa at pangarap
Pigilin ang mga nawawalang bahagi
At makahanap ng kahulugan
Sa mga nawawalang damdamin
O, magtiis tayo upang pahalagahan
Ang isang regalo
Halika ang magandang gabi ay nakalulugod.

# TRANSLATION

# ON

# A

# GIFT 1II

# A GIFT III

Petals are artless to the eyes
Dots rule their innermost being and
Forsaken with the aromatic smell
Like falling leaves that are
Diverse in size and shape without their
typical budding point and smell
But its beauty and essence lie from within
And you, a Gift
like
Petals and leaves whose essence
springs from its bosom—

Endless

like water in the ocean
Ceaselessly musing and inspiring
As the beauty from within
Shines the brightest and
Keeps on shining its bright

# PANGASINENSE TRANSLATION
By John Flores


# SAY REGALON KUMATLO

Saray pisag na rosas gapoy para ed mata
Say malimpek a bokel makauley ed inkasikato san
Tinaynanan ya walay maabig ya angub
Singa napapattak iran bulong a
Aliwaliwa ran kabaleg tan utsoy anggapo iray
Tugtuwan isimit to tan angub
Balet say gana tan gamor to wadjad loob
San sika, say Regalo
Singa
Pisag na rosas tan bulong ya say gamor
Nanlapod ed ulnos to –

Gapoy unor
Singa danum ed dayat
Anggapoy angaan ya dakep tan ligliwa
Singa gana ed loob
Unliliwawan maung san
Leneg ya manliwawa ed pinakaliwawa

## TAGALOG TRANSLATION
### Zaldy F. Perez

# ANG PANGATLONG REGALO

Ang mga talutot ay walang halaga sa mga mata
Punong puno ng mga anuntunan ng kanilang panloob na
kagandahan
At pinabayaan ng mabangong amoy
Tulad ng pagbagsak ng mga dahon
Magkakaibang hugis  at laki
Nang wala ang kanilang tipikal na usbong at amoy
Ngunit ang kagandahan at kakanyahan nito
Ay namamalagi sa loob
At ikaw, isang regalo
Tulad ng mga talutot at dahon
Na ang kakanyahang bukal mula sa walang katapusan
Tulad ng tubig sa dagat
Walang tigil sa pagbibigay ng inspirasyon
Bilang kagandahang  mula sa loob
Nagliliwanag ng pinakamaliwanag
At patuloy na nagniningning nang pinakamaliwanag.

# TRANSLATION

# ON

# A

# GIFT 1V

# A GIFT IV

The raging storms in life ---
hostile wind that brings sting
raindrops during the cloudiest hours
thunder and lightning rupturing
from the heart breaking.

The storms that gave birth to these rivers
drowning
the broken hearts and lost souls
But a Gift bridles the lost course and
Gives life to the dying soul.

A Gift,  brilliant as a diamond
Life's treasure that is priceless
No storms can dim its luster
perfected through trust and respect
more matured minds and
enduring hearts
can understand

# PANGASINENSE TRANSLATION
By John Flores


# SAY REGALON KUMAPAT

say maksil ya guemguem na bilay ---
makapagan dagem awit toy paga
tayaketek na uran ed makulemlem ya oras
karol tan kirmat mamapasnuk
lapud say puson asakitan.


Saray guemguem ya angiyanak ed sarayan ilog
Nalelegep
say puson asakitan tan abalang a imanu
Balet say Regalo tundaan na abalang a imanu san
Iter bilay ed umpapatey a imanu/kamarerwa
Say Regalo, marlang singa dyamante
Kayamanan na bilay ya mabli
Gapoy guemguem ya makapanpabilunget na
inkasikato
inapipiger ed tiwala tan respeto
mas matakken na kanunutan tan
matepel a puso
makatalos

# TAGALOG TRANSLATION
By Zaldy F. Perez

# ANG PANG APAT NA REGALO

Ang matinding unos sa buhay
Pagalit na hangin na nagdudulot ng kirot
Patak ng ulan sa panahon ng pagsubok
Sa oras ng kulog at kidlat
Mula sa pusong durog
Ang mga unos ay nabubuong malunod
Ang mga nawawalang puong wasak
Ngunit ang isang relago ay nakapigil
At nagbibigay pag-asa sa mga namamatay na damdamin
Isang regalo, maningning bilang isang brilyante
Kayamanan ng buhay na walang katumbas ng anumang
halaga
Walang anumang unos na maaaring
Makapagpalabo ng kanyang kinang
Naging perpekto sa pamamagitan ng tiwala at respeto
Ang tamang isip
Naiintindihan ang walang hanggang pagtibok ng puso.

# TRANSLATION

# ON

# A

# GIFT V

# A Gift V

As I gaze upon the sky
I see the beautiful memories of
A wonderful friendship that
Stands through the test of time

I see the wandering clouds
Being pushed by the hostile wind
Resilient and forming a rain
Refreshing to the soul.

I see the birds enjoying their liberty
Soaring at their greater heights
No matter what life's struggle
A Gift will always be the wind beneath their wings.

I see the sun with its brilliant rays
Which continues to shine at its brightest
No matter how strong the storms may be
A Gift will be its strength forever.

# PANGASINENSE TRANSLATION
By John Flores

**SAY REGALON KUMALIMA**

Nu untatangay a ked tawen
Nanengneng ko su marakep ya agatgawa
Say makapakelaw ya pipiyulop ya
Inmalagey jad subok na panaun

Anengneng ko su panaakar na ulap
Itutulak na maksil a dagem
Matalunggaring san unuuksoy ya uran
Makapaligliway imanun inkatoo.

Nanengneng ko iray siwit anamit day inawa
Mantekyab ed sankatageyan
Angganu anton klasen guyayem ed bilay
Say Regalo siyansya yan dagem anggad leksab na aray
pakpak da.

Nanengneng ko su agew ya walay marling ton sinag
Ya mangipapatuloy unliwawa ed pinakaliwawa
Annganu ganun ton kakasil tan su guemguem
Say Regalo siyansyan mabiskeg anggad kapigan.

# TAGALOG TRANSLATION
By Zaldy F. Perez

# ANG PANG LIMANG REGALO

Habang tumitingin ako sa langit
Nakikita ko ang mga magagandang ala-ala
Na isang magandang pagkakaibigan
Na nalampasan ang pagsubok ng panahon

Nakikita ko ang alapaap
Tinutulak ng pagalit na hangin
Matatag at bumubuo ng ulan
Napakasapa sa aking damdamin

Nakikita ko ang mga ibon na tinatamasa ang kanilang
Kalayaan
Pumailanglang sa pinakamataas
Kahit anumang pakikibaksa sa buhay
Isang regalo ang palaging magtutulak sa ilalim ng kanilang
mga pakpak

Nakikita ko ang araw na nakakasilaw ang kanyang sinag
Na patuloy itong lumiliwanag
Kahit gaanuman kabigat ang unos
Isang regalo ang magiging lakas magpakailanman.

# TRANSLATION

# ON

# A

# GIFT 5- SERIES

# IN

# INTERNATIONAL

# LANGUAGES

# TRANSLATION

# ON

# A

# GIFT 1

# A GIFT

You've inspired me more than anybody else
To strive for more learning and improve my craft
You've shown me how to be competent
And to remain humble despite
countless achievements.

Days will never be the same again
Without your friendship in my life
They called you a star, but I call you a diamond
Who shines brightly by showing other people's
worth.

Days in this lifetime will never be enough
To show my appreciation of a God-given gift
Perfectly wrapped with overflowing talents and
wisdom--
An ullassa that I dreamed of someday.

I know it is too much to request
To please promise me to always be around
No matter how hard it is
No matter what it takes
For I shall dwell and
Walk in our friendship forever

## ALBANIAN TRANSLATION
By Sherife Allko

# NJË DHURATË

Ju më keni frymëzuar më shumë se kushdo tjetër
Të përpiqem për më shumë të mësuar dhe për të përmirësuar
zanatin tim
Ju më keni treguar se si të jem kompetent
Dhe të mbetet i përulur pavarësisht
arritje të panumërta.

Ditët nuk do të jenë më të njëjtat
Pa miqësinë tënde në jetën time
Ata ju quajtën një yll, por unë ju quaj një diamant
Kush shkëlqen shkëlqyeshëm duke treguar ato të njerëzve të
tjerë
me vlerë

Ditët në këtë jetë nuk do të jenë kurrë të mjaftueshme
Për të treguar vlerësimin tim për një dhuratë të dhënë nga
Zoti
E mbështjellë në mënyrë perfekte me talente të tejmbushura
dhe
mençuri -
Një ullassa që ëndërroja një ditë.

E di që është shumë për të kërkuar
Të lutem më premto që të jem gjithmonë pranë
Pavarësisht se sa e vështirë është
Pavarësisht se çfarë duhet,
Sepse unë do të banoj dhe
Ecni në miqësinë tonë përgjithmonë

# ASSAMESE TRANSLATION
By Malakshmi Borthakur

## এটি উপহাৰ

তুমিয়েই মোক সকলোতকৈ অধিক প্ৰেৰণা দি আহিছা,
যাতে মই অধিক জ্ঞান আহৰণ কৰিবলৈ আগ্ৰহী হওঁ,
যাতে মই মোৰ শিল্পকৰ্মত উন্নতি কৰিবলৈ অহোপুৰুষাৰ্থ কৰোঁ,
তুমি মোক শিকালা নিপুণতাৰ পাঠ !
আৰু শিকালা অসংখ্য প্ৰাপ্তিৰ পিছতো কিদৰে বিনম্ৰ হ'ব লাগে
!


তোমাৰ বন্ধুত্বৰ অবিহনে মোৰ দিনবোৰ আৰু কেতিয়াও
আগৰ দৰে হৈ নাথাকিব !
সিঁতে তোমাক ৰিজাইছিল তৰাৰ লগত !
কিন্তু মোৰ মানত তুমি এটুকুৰা হীৰা !
যি উজ্জ্বল হৈ জিলিকে,
আনৰ যোগ্যতাক উচিত মূল্য প্ৰদান কৰি !


মোৰ এই জীৱনটো যথেষ্ট নহয়
প্ৰতিভা আৰু বুদ্ধিমত্তাৰে ওপচ খাই থকা
এটি ঈশ্বৰপ্ৰদত্ত উপহাৰৰ প্ৰশংসা কৰিবলৈ
ই এটি উল্লাস, যিটো মোৰ বাবে এক সপোন মাথোঁ !


মই জানোঁ, মই অধিক বিচাৰিছোঁ তোমাৰ পৰা
যে মোক কথা দিয়া তুমি সদায় মোৰ কাষত থাকিবা !
এই কাম যিমানেই কঠিন নহওঁক কিয় !
আৰু ইয়াৰ প্ৰতিদান যিয়েই নহওঁক কিয়  !
এই বন্ধুত্বতেই মোৰ বসতি হ'ব

এই বন্ধুত্বতেই মই বিচৰণ কৰিম,  চিৰদিন

# BENGALI TRANSLATION
### By Queen Sarkar

# একটি উপহার

আপনি অন্য কারও চেয়ে আমাকে অনুপ্রাণিত
করেছেন
আরও শিখার জন্য প্রচেষ্টা এবং আমার নৈপুণ্য
উন্নত করার জন্য,
কীভাবে সক্ষম হতে হবে তা আপনি আমাকে
দেখিয়েছেন
এবং অগনিত কৃতিত্বের পরেও
আপনি নম্রতা শিখিয়েছেন

দিন আর কখনও একই হবে না
আমার জীবনে আপনার বন্ধুত্ব ছাড়া
তারা আপনাকে তারকা বলেছিল, কিন্তু আমি
আপনাকে হীরা বলেছি
যিনি অন্য লোককে দেখিয়ে উজ্জ্বলভাবে উজ্জ্বল
হন।

এই জীবনকালের দিনগুলি কখনই পর্যাপ্ত হবে না

ঈশ্বর প্রদত্ত উপহারের জন্য আমার উপলব্ধি
প্রকাশ করার জন্য
পুরোপুরি উপচে পড়া প্রতিভা এবং
জ্ঞান
আমি একটি দিন স্বপ্ন দেখেছি একটি উল্লাসের।


আমি জানি এটি অনুরোধ করা খুব বেশি কঠীন
আমাকে সবসময় আশেপাশে থাকার প্রতিশ্রুতি
দিন
তা যতই কষ্টকর হোক না কেন
যাই লাগে না কেন
আমি বাস করব
চিরকাল আমাদের বন্ধুত্বে

# BRAZILIAN TRANSLATION
By Shakil Kalam

## Um presente-1

Você me inspirou mais do que qualquer
outra pessoa. Aprender mais,
Esforce-se e melhore meu ofício.
Você me mostrou como ser capaz e
humildemente realizar inúmeros.

Meu dia nunca mais será o mesmo,
Preciso mais da sua amizade na minha vida.
Eles te chamam de estrela,
Mas eu sei que você é um diamante.
Quem ele mesmo com a riqueza de outro homem
Quer brilhar; Isso nunca é possível.

Os dias desta vida nunca serão suficientes
Transbordando talento e expressar minha
gratidão pelos dons dados por Deus Encerre com
sabedoria -
Sonhei com um êxtase um dia.

Vou fazer um pedido, para prometer que
estará por perto o tempo todo Será –
não importa o quão difícil seja ou
o que quer que seja. Você tem que fazer isso.
Eu vou viver; Nossa amizade durará para sempre.

# DARI TRANSLATION
## By Parwez Hashimi

# ‫حفه اول‬

آنها هرگز شما را به یک ستاره نمی شناسم ، اما من شما
روزهای زندگی در این زندگی هرگز    .را به الماس می گویم
کافی نخواهند بود تا قدردانی خود را از یک هدیه خدادادی نشان
.دهم که کاملاً با استعدادهای سرشار و خرد پیچیده شده است


من می دانم که درخواست بیش از حد بسیار
زیاد است لطفاً به من قول دهید که همیشه در اطرافم باشم هر
چقدر هم سخت باشد مهم نیست چه چیزی طول می کشد زیرا من
ساکن و پیاده خواهم شد

# GUJARATI TRANSLATION
By Bhanubhai Patel

# ભેટ।

વધુ શીખવા માટે પ્રયત્ન કરવા અને મારી કળાને
સુધારવા માટે તમે મને બીજા કોઈ કરતા વધારે
પ્રેરણા આપી છેતમે મને કેવી રીતે સક્ષમ
થવું અને અસંખ્ય સિદ્ધિઓ હોવા છતાં
નમ્ર કેમ રહેવું તે બતાવ્યું છે.
દિવસો ફરી ક્યારેય સરખા રહેશે નહીં
તમારી મિત્રતા વિના મારા જીવનમાં
તેઓએ તમને એક તારો કહ્યો, પણ હું તમને હીરો કહું છું જે અન્ય
લોકોના મૂલ્યબતાવીને તેજસ્વી રીતે ચમકતો હોય છે.

આ જીવનકાળમાં દિવસો ક્યારેય પૂરતા રહેશે નહી ભગવાન
દ્વારા આપવામાં આવેલી છલકાતી પ્રતિભાઓ અને ડહાપણથી
સંપૂર્ણ રીતે આવરિત ભેટની મારી કદર બતાવવા
માટે ---
મેં કોઈ દિવસ સપનું જોયું તે ઉલ્લસા.

હું જાણું છું કે વિનંતી કરવી ઘણી વધારે છે
કૃપા કરીને મને હંમેશાં આસપાસ રહેવાનું વચન આપો

ભલે તે ગમે તેટલું મુશ્કેલ હોય ભલે તે
ગમે તેટલો ભોગ માગેતેના માટે
હું રહીશ અનેઅમારી મિત્રતામાં
કાયમ ચાલીશ

# PASHTO TRANSLATION
By Parwez Hashimi


## تحفه(دالۍ)لومړنی

تا له بل هر چا څخه زه ډير هڅولی )لمسولی(یمه،ترڅو د نورو زده کړه لپاره هڅه وکړم او خپل هنر ته پرمختگ ورکړم او د نفرت په مقابل کی عاجز)متواضع)پاتی شم،بی حسابه لاسته راوړنی.

ستا له ملگرتیا پرته به بیا هیڅکله ورځي زما په ژوند کی داسي نه وي.

هغوي تاته ستوری وايي،خو زه تاته الماس هغه الماس کوم چی نورو ته د غلطو په بڼودلو سره څلیږي.

د ژوند په دی وخت کی به ورځي هیڅکله کافي نه وي تر څو خپله مننه وبنایم د خدای د طرفه راکړل شوی دالۍ څخه.

په مکمله توگه رانغاړلی د استعدادونو او حکمت څخه یو طبیعي خوشحالي چی د بعضو ورځو لپاره یي ما خوب لیدلی.

زه پوهیږم دا ډير زیات دي چی زه یي درخواست وکړم.

خو هیله ماسره دا وعده وکړه چی همیشه به زما شاوخوا اوسي که هر څه پیښنیږي،زه باید همیشه زموږ په ملگرتیا کی اوسم او همیشه یوځای وگرځو.

# PUNJABI TRANSLATION
## By Mohit Katyal

# ਇਕ ਉਪਹਾਰ - 1

ਮੈ ਤੇਰੇ ਤੋਂ ਅੱਗੇ ਵਧਣ ਦਾ ਸਲੀਕਾ ਸਿੱਖਿਆ..
ਮੈ ਤੇਰੇ ਤੋਂ ਲੜਨ ਦਾ ਤਰੀਕਾ ਸਿੱਖਿਆ..
ਤੂੰ ਮੈਨੂੰ ਹਮੇਸ਼ਾ ਜ਼ਮੀਨ ਤੇ ਰਹਿਣ ਦੀ ਜਾਚ ਦਿਤੀ..
ਭਾਵੇਂ ਮੇਰੇ ਕੋਲ ਹੈ ਜਹਾਨ ਜਿਤਿਆ..

ਮੈਨੂੰ ਪਤਾ ਹੈ..
ਤੇਰੇ ਬਿਨਾ ਮੇਰੀ ਜ਼ਿੰਦਗੀ ਚ ਬਾਹਰ ਨਹੀਂ ਆਉਣੀ..
ਉਹ ਭਾਵੇਂ ਤੈਨੂੰ ਤਾਰਾ ਕਹਿਣ ..
ਪਰ ਮੇਰੇ ਲਈ ਤੂੰ ਅਜੀਹਾ ਹੀਰਾ ਹੈ..
ਜਿਸਦੀ ਚਮਕ ਦੁਸਰਿਆਂ ਨੂੰ ਉਹਨਾਂ ਦੀ ਕੀਮਤ ਦਸਦੀ ਹੈ ..

ਇਹ ਜ਼ਿੰਦਗੀ ਸ਼ਾਇਦ ਅਜਿਹੀ ਸ਼ਾਮ ਲੈ ਆਵੇ..
ਮੈ ਪੁਰੀ ਤਰਾ ਤੇਰੇ ਆਉਣ ਦਾ ਸ਼ੁਕਰਗੁਜ਼ਾਰ ਕਰ ਸਕਾ..

ਮੇਨੂ ਪਤਾ ਹੈ, ਮੈ ਬਹੁਤ ਜ਼ਿਆਦਾ ਮੰਗਿਆ ਹੈ ..
ਤੇਰਾ ਹਰ ਪਲ ਮੇਰੇ ਕੋਲ ਰਹਿਣ ਦੇ ਲਈ..
ਮੈ ਸਬ ਹਾਰ ਜਾਵਾਂ..
ਹਰ ਹੱਦ ਤੋਂ ਗੁਜ਼ਰ ਜਾਵਾਂ..
ਤੇਰੇ ਨਾਲ ਇਸ ਸਫਰ ਵਿਚ ਜਾਣ ਦੇ ਲਈ..

# SETSWANA TRANSLATION
By Kenneth Maswabi

## Mpho (karolo ya ntlha)


O ntshenoletse masaitsiweng a botshelo go feta
botlhe
Go leba mo boteng jwa thuto le go tlhabolola tiro
yame
O ntshupegeditse tsela ya go nna mmampudi
Go itshetlela mo moeng wa setho
Ke sa sirwa ke se ke se kgonneng mo botshelong


Malatsi a botshelo ga a kitla a tshwana gape
Kontle ga botsalano jwa gago mo botshelong jwa me
Bane ba go bitsa naledi, mme nna ke go bitsa
teemane
Ee galalelang go supa bokgone jwa batho ba bangwe


Malatsi a botshelo ga a ketla a nna mantsi
Go supa tshiamelo (Mpho) e ke e filweng ke
Modimo
Ee bofilweng ka dikitsokitso le botlhaletlhale
Bontlenyane jo ke bolorileng mo letsatsing lengwe
Ke a itse gore kopo yame e feteletse
Mme fela ke kopa gore o mpate ka malatsi otlhe
Le fa go le thata
Le ka sengwe le sengwe sese tlhokafalang
Ka jalo ke itshepisitse go tsamaya mo botsalanong
jwa rona goya goileng

# TAMIL TRANSLATION
By Radhakrishan Krishnan

## ஒரு பரிசு

கல்வியினால் என் திறமையை
அதிகரிக்க

நீ மற்றவர்களை விட என் அகத்தை
அதிகமாக தூண்டினாய்

நீ எனக்கு மேலும் தகுதி அடைய வழி
காட்டினாய்

எண்ணமுடியாத வெற்றிகள்
அடைந்தபோதிலும்

அடக்கமாக இருக்க கற்றுத்தந்தாய்

உன் நட்பு இல்லாமல்
என் வாழ்க்கையில் நாட்கள்
மீண்டும் ஒருபோல இருக்காது
அவர்கள் உன்னை நக்ஷத்திரம் என்று
அழைத்தார்கள்

ஆனால் நான் உமை வைரம் என்று
அழைப்பேன்

நீ மற்றவர்களுக்கு வழி காட்டும்
விளக்கு போல மிழில்கிறாய்.


இந்த இறை கொடுத்த பரிசை மதிப்பிட
என் வாழ்க்கையின் நாட்கள் போதேவே
போதாது

இந்த அருமையான நட்பென்னும்
பரிசை அடைய

நான் மிக நாட்கள் கனவு கொண்டேன்


எத்தனை கடினமாலனும்

எத்தனை சோதனை வந்தாலும்

எப்பொழுதும் கூடவே இருக்க
உறுதியளி

நானும் உன் இதயத்தில்
வசிந்துகொண்டு

நட்பின் பாதையில் வலம் வருவேன்

# TELUGO TRANSLATION
By Rama Krishna Perugo

## ఒక బహుమతి I

మీరు నన్ను అందరికంటే ఎక్కువగా ప్రేరేపించారు
మరింత నేర్చుకోవడానికి కృషి చేయడానికి
మరియు నా నైపుణ్యాన్ని మెరుగుపరచడానికి
సమర్థుడిగా ఎలా ఉండాలో మీరు నాకు చూపించారు
మరియు వినయంగా ఉండటానికి
లెక్కలేనన్ని విజయాలు.

రోజులు మరలా ఒకేలా ఉండవు
నా జీవితంలో మీ స్నేహం లేకుండా
వారు మిమ్మల్ని ఒక నక్షత్రం అని పిలిచారు,
కాని నేను నిన్ను వజ్రం అని పిలుస్తాను
ఇతరులను చూపించడం ద్వారా
ఎవరు ప్రకాశవంతంగా ప్రకాశిస్తారు
విలువ.

ఈ జీవితకాలంలో రోజులు ఎప్పటికీ సరిపోవు
దేవుడు ఇచ్చిన బహుమతి పట్ల నా ప్రశంసలను
చూపించడానికి
పొంగిపొర్లుతున్న ప్రతిభతో చక్కగా చుట్టబడి ఉంటుంది
జ్ఞానం -
నేను ఏదో ఒక రోజు కలలు కన్న ఉల్లాసా.

అభ్యర్థించడం చాలా ఎక్కువ అని నాకు తెలుసు
దయచేసి ఎల్లప్పుడూ చుట్టూ ఉండాలని నాకు హామీ
ఇవ్వండి
ఎంత కష్టపడినా
ఏమి తీసుకున్నా సరే

# VIETNAMESE TRANSLATION
## By HONG NGOC CHAU

# MỘT MÓN QUÀ

Cảm hứng cho tôi bạn đã gửi
Nhiều hơn bất cứ những ai kia
Cùng nhau phấn đấu và trao đổi
Học hỏi nhiều hơn, cải thiện nghề.

Bạn chỉ cho tôi tạo thực lực
Sẵn sàng tiến bước khi đua tranh
Vẫn luôn  khiêm tốn dù thành tích
Vô số bài thơ đã đạt thành

Ngày sẽ không bao giờ trở lại
Thời gian như cũ ở trong đời
Mà tôi có thể thiếu tình bạn
Tiểu bạn trong cuộc sống của tôi

Họ gọi bạn là sao Bắc đẩu
Nhưng tôi gọi bạn là kim cương
Sáng ngời giá trị cho người thấy
So sánh không chi rực rỡ bằng

Sẽ chẳng bao giờ có thể đủ
Đủ ngày đủ tháng đủ thời gian
Để tôi đánh giá cao công trạng
Một món quà do Thiên Chúa ban

Hoàn hảo tài năng và trí tuệ
Tràn trề sáng tạo và khôn ngoan
Ullassa đó tôi mơ ước
Sẽ  được một ngày tôi hợp đoàn

Tôi biết điều này quá ước vọng
Quá nhiều tha thiết khi yêu cầu
Với tôi hãy hứa luôn bên cạnh
Xin bạn vui lòng đến với nhau

Dù có khó khăn cho đến mấy
Chúng ta không có vấn đề gì
Vì tôi ở  mãi trong tình bạn
Tình của chúng ta không chuyển di.

# TRANSLATION

# ON

# A

# GIFT II

# A GIFT II

The sky is bright and gay
Night is bejeweled with enchanting stars with
the moon and its beautifully crafted trenches


From afar, the chirping crickets are pleasing to the
ears
Creating a loquacious night till the break of dawn.
Come, the beautiful night is pleading
Let us drink the water that
Runs to the rivers that mend
broken hearts and souls.
Oh, let us endure to treasure
a Gift that seems to disappear but is
still breathing and continuing to
give life to the broken hopes and dreams
Bridle the lost course and
find meaning to lost soul.
Oh! Let us endure to treasure a Gift
Come the beautiful night is pleading.

# ALBANIAN TRANSLATION
By Sherife Allko

# Një DHURAT II

Qielli është i ndritshëm dhe homoseksual
Nata është zbukuruar me yje magjepsës me
hëna dhe llogoret e saj të krijuara bukur

Nga larg, crikicat e cicërimave janë të këndshme për
veshët
Krijimi i një nate të butë deri në agimin e agimit.
Eja, nata e bukur po përgjërohet
Le të pimë ujin që
Vrapon drejt lumenjve që rregullohen
zemrat dhe shpirtrat e thyer.
Oh, le të durojmë në thesar
një dhuratë që duket se zhduket por është
ende merr frymë dhe vazhdon të
jepi jetë shpresave dhe ëndrrave të thyera
Bridle kursin e humbur dhe
gjeni kuptim për shpirtin e humbur.
Oh!  Le të durojmë të çmojmë një Dhuratë
Eja nata e bukur po përgjërohet

# ASSAMESE TRANSLATION
By Malakshmi Borthakur

## এটি উপহাৰ (২)

আকাশখন আজি উজ্জ্বল আৰু প্ৰফুল্লিত
নিশাজনীয়েও আজি নিজকে সজাইছে
চিকমিকাই থকা তৰাৰ গহনা,
আৰু জোনত খোদিত ছিদ্ৰবোৰেৰে মীনা কৰা সাজটিৰে !

দূৰৰ পৰা ভাঁহি অহা উইচিৰিঙাৰ মাতবোৰ কাণত সুমধুৰ
হৈ ধৰা দিছে
ইঁতে নিশাক আজি দোকমোকালিলৈকে প্ৰগলভ কৰি ৰাখিব !
আহাঁচোন ! এক সুন্দৰ নিশাৰ অনুৰোধ এয়া !
ব'লা ! আমি সৌ বৈ থকা নৈ কেইখনিৰ পানী খাওঁ
সেই পানী খালে হেনো টুকুৰা টুকুৰ হৈ যোৱা
হৃদয় আৰু আত্মাবিলাক পুনৰাই জোৰা লাগে !
আহাঁচোন ! অলপ যন্ত্ৰণা সহি হ'লেও এটি উপহাৰক সঞ্চিত
কৰি ৰাখোঁ !
যি দৃশ্যমান নহ'লেও সৰ্বত্ৰে ব্যাপ্ত
যি খণ্ড-বিখণ্ড হোৱা আশাবোৰ আৰু সপোনবোৰক জীৱন দি
আহিছে
যিয়ে ছন্দ হেৰুৱাই পেলোৱা জীৱনৰ শৃংখলাটোক সামৰি ৰাখে
যিয়ে লুপ্তপ্ৰায় আত্মাবিলাকক পুনৰোজ্জীৱিত কৰে
আহাচোন ! অলপ যন্ত্ৰণা সহি হ'লেও  এটি উপহাৰক সঞ্চিত
কৰি ৰাখোঁ !
এক সুন্দৰ নিশাৰ অনুৰোধ এয়া !

# BENGALI TRANSLATION
## By Queen Sarkar

# একটি উপহার ॥

আকাশটি উজ্জ্বল এবং ধূসর
রাতটি মন্ত্রমুগ্ধ চাঁদ তারকাদের সাথে
সুন্দর কারুকার্য করা


দূর থেকে চিরচেনা ঝিঁঝি পোকার ডাক মণ কে প্রসন্ন করছে
ভোর বিরতি অবধি এক কথনামুলক রাত তৈরি করছে।
এসো, সুন্দর রাতটি মিনতি করছে
আমরা সেই জল পান করি,
যা ভগ্ন হৃদয় এবং আত্মা কে শান্তি দেয়।
আমাদের এই অমুল্য রতন কে যত্ন করা উচিত
এইটি একটা এমন উপহার যা অদৃশ্য বলে মনে হয়
কিন্তু এইটি
ভাঙ্গা আশা এবং স্বপ্ন কে জীবন দেয়।
হারানো পথ কে ভুলে
হারানো আত্মার অর্থ সন্ধান করুন।
উহু! আসুন আমরা এই উপহারকে মূল্যবান বলে মনে করি
আসুন সুন্দর রাতটি মিনতি করছে।

# BRAZILIAN TRANSLATION
By Shakil Kalam


## Um presente-2


O céu está claro e alegre
A noite se torna fascinante com a lua e
ressoa com as estrelas,
E seu belo design de trincheira.
O chilrear dos grilos ecoa nos ouvidos de longe;
Soprou sem parar até o amanhecer,
criando uma noite catastrófica.


Venha, desejando a bela noite, bebamos a
água que correm os rios; Essa água
purifica ocoração e a alma quebrantados.


Ah! Nós valorizamos este presente invisível.
Que ainda está respirando e constantemente
revivendo esperanças e sonhos quebrados.
Feche o caminho perdido e busque o significado da
Alma perdida.
Vamos orar por uma bela noite.
Dar vida
Pare o caminho perdido e
Encontre significado na alma perdida.


Vamos valorizar o presente
Vamos tornar a bela noite alegre.

# DARI TRANSLATION
By Parwez Hashimi


تحفه دوهم:-

آسمان روشن است و همجنسگرا شب با ستاره ها و
سنگرهای زیبایی ساخته شده آن از ستاره های دلربا
مجذوب می شود.
از دور ، جیرجیرک های دلپذیر برای گوش خشنود هستند
و یک شب آرام و طوفانی تا طلوع آفتاب ایجاد می کنند . بیا
شب زیبا با ادعای ،    بگذار آب ما را به رودخانه هایی که,
، قلب و روح شکسته را اصلاح می کنند ، بنوشیم . اوه
بگذارید تحمل کنیم گنج
هدیه ای که به نظر می رسد ناپدید می شود اما هنوز نفس
می کشد و زندگی خود را به امیدها و آرزوهای شکسته
ادامه می دهد.


مسیر گمشده را مرتب کنید و به روح گمشده معنی دهید . اوه
بگذارید تحمل کنیم که یک هدیه را گنج کنیم ، بیا شب
زیبایی استعلام می کند.
-----------------------

# GUJARATI TRANSLATION
By Bhanubhai Patel

# ભેટ ॥

આકાશ તેજસ્વી અને ભૂખરુ છે
રાત્રી  ચંદ્ર અને આભૂષણ જડિત મોહક તારાઓ સાથે
સુશોભિત છે અને દ્રરની તેની  સુંદર રચાયેલ ખાઈઓ

કાનને ખુશ કરી દે તેવો તમરાનો અવાજ પરોઢિયાં સુધી
વાચાળ રાત્રીનું સર્જન કરે છે.  આવો, સુંદર રાત્રી
વિનંતી કરે છે ચાલો આપણે તે પાણી પીએ
જે  નદીઓ તરફ દોડે છે જે
તૂટેલા હ્રદય અને આત્માઓને
દુરસ્ત કરે છે.
ઓહ, એ ભેટને જતન કરવાનો પ્રયત્ન
કરીએ જે અદ્રશ્ય થતી લાગે પણ હજી
તે જીવંત છે અને તૂટેલા સપનાઓ અને આશાઓને
જાન આપે છે ખોવાયેલ પાથને લગામ આપે છે
ખોવાયેલ આત્માને અર્થ આપે છે.
ઓહ!  ચાલો આપણે એ ભેટનું જતન
કરીએ આવો સુંદર રાત્રિ વિનંતી કરે છે.

# PASHTO TRANSLATION
## By Parwez Hashimi

# دوهمه دالۍ_A

اسمان روبنانه دی او ځلانده شپه د زړه ورونکو ستورو او سپوږمی پواسطه سینګار شوی .دا په بنایسته توګه مورچلونه فاسدوي.

له لیري،د چرچر اوازونه غوږونو ته خوشحالي ورکوي د شورماشور ډکي شپي په منځته راوړلو سره تر سباوون پوري.

راشه، دا بنایسته شپه درخواست کوي،راځه هغه اوبه وڅکو چی په سیندونو کی رواني دي کوم چی مات زړونه او خاوره (جوړوي)رغوي.

اوه!موږ ته اجازه راکړه چی وزغمو،تر څو هغه تحفه وژغورو کومه چی د فناء کیدو په حال کی ده خو اوس هم ساه اخلي او ماتو هیلو او خوبونو ته ژوند ورکوي.

کړې او مخکیني روح ته معنا bridle مخکیني کورسونه پیداکړی.

اوه!موږ ته اجازه راکړی چی وزغمو،ترڅوخوندي کړو هغه تحفه چی دا بنایسته شپه یي درخواست کوي.

**PUNJABI TRANSLATION**
By Mohit Katyal

# ਇਕ ਉਪਹਾਰ - 2

ਅਸਮਾਨ ਚਮਕਦਾਰ ਅਤੇ ਸੁਹਾਨਾ ਹੈ

ਰਾਤ ਮਨਮੋਹਕ ਤਾਰਿਆਂ ਨਾਲ ਜਗਮਗ ਹੈ

ਚੰਨ ਅਤੇ ਇਸ ਦੀਆਂ ਖੁਬਸੁਰਤ ਇਹ ਖਾਈਆਂ

ਦੂਰੋਂ ਹੀ, ਚਿੜਕਦੀਆਂ, ਕੰਨ ਅਤੇ ਮਨ ਪ੍ਰਸੰਨ ਕਰ ਰਹੀਆਂ ਹਨ

ਸਵੇਰ ਦੇ ਇਤੰਜਾਰ ਵਿੱਚ ਇਕ ਕਮਜ਼ੋਰ ਰਾਤ ਬਣਾ ਰਹੀਆਂ
ਹਨ

ਵੇਖੇ ਕਿਵੇਂ , ਰਾਤ ਬੇਨਤੀ ਕਰ ਰਹੀ ਹੈ

ਚਲੋ ਉਹ ਪਾਣੀ ਪੀ ਲਈਏ ਜੋ

ਸੁੱਕਦੀਆਂ ਰੂਹਾਂ ਨੂੰ ਨਦੀਆਂ ਵੱਲ ਭੇਜਦੀ ਹੈ

ਸਾਨੂੰ ਇਸ ਖਜ਼ਾਨੇ ਨੂੰ ਸਾਂਭਣਾ ਚਾਹੀਦਾ ਹੈ

ਅਜਿਹਾ ਉਪਹਾਰ ਕਦੇ ਅਲੋਪ ਹੁੰਦਾ ਜਾਪਦਾ ਹੈ

ਪਰ, ਅਜੇ ਵੀ ਜਿਉਂਦਾ ਅਤੇ ਜਾਰੀ ਹੈ

ਟੁੱਟੀਆਂ ਉਮੀਦਾਂ ਅਤੇ ਸੁਪਨਿਆਂ ਨੂੰ ਜ਼ਿੰਦ ਦਈਏ

ਗੁੰਮ ਗਏ ਰਸਤੇ ਤੋ ਮੁੜ

ਗੁਆਚੀ ਰੂਹ ਦਾ ਮਤਲਬ ਲੱਭੀਏ.

ਆਓ! ਇੱਕ ਉਪਹਾਰ ਨੂੰ ਅਨਮੋਲ ਕਰ ਲਈਏ

ਆਓ, ਰਾਤ ਬੇਨਤੀ ਕਰ ਰਹੀ ਹੈ.

# SETSWANA TRANSLATION
By Kenneth Maswabi

## Mpho (karolo ya bobedi)

Loapi lo apere phatsimo le boitumelo
Bosigo bo apesitswe lesire la dinaledi
Ngwedi le yone gotlhe le mantlenyane a mesima ya
yone

Mobokgakaleng, dikhukhwane di opela bontle jo bo
makatsang tsebe
Go bopa bosigo jo botletseng dipuisanyo
Tlang kwano, bosigo jo bontle boa lo laletsa
Tlang re nwe metsi a elelang go ya nokeng
Ee hapisang dipelo tse dibotlhoko
A reithuteng go tlhokomela
Mpho ee lebegang etla nyelela
Mme fela e tsweletse ka go hema
Le go fa botshelo mo go tsotlhe tse di senang
tshepho
Le ditoro tota
Tsenya ditomo mo tseleng ee latlhegileng
Mme o tla tshela boamaaruri mo moyeng oo
latlhegileng
A re ithuteng go tlhokomela mpho e
Tlang kwano, bosigo jo bontle boa lo laletsa

# TAMIL TRANSLATION
By Radhakrishan Krishnan

## ஒரு பரிசு II

உவகையுள்ள ஒளிமயமான வானம்,
இரவு, மயக்கும் நக்ஷத்திரங்களையும்,
நிலவையும்
ஆபரணமாக அணிந்துகொண்டது.
தூரத்தில் சில்வண்டுகள் கீச்சிடும்
ஓசை
காதுக்கு இனிமையாக இருந்தது
அவைகள் விடியும்வரை
ஒரு ஓசையுள்ள இரவை
உண்டாக்கின

வா , அழகான இரவு அழைக்கிறது
நாம் வாழ்க்கை என்ற நதியின் நீரை
அருந்தி
உடைந்த இதயத்தையும்,
ஆத்மாவையும் பழுது செய்வோம்
நாம் அந்த விலையில்லாத பரிசை

ஒர் செல்வம் போல் பாதுகார்க்போம்
அந்த பரிசு உடைந்த
நம்பிக்கைகளுக்கும் கனவுகளுக்கும்
உயிர் கொடுத்து, தொலைந்த
பாதைக்கு
வழிகாட்டி, காணாமல் போன
ஆத்மாவின் பொருள் உறைய
உதவட்டும்

நாம் அந்த விலையில்லாத பரிசை
ஒர் செல்வம் போல் பாதுகார்க்போம்

வா , அழகான இரவு அழைக்கிறது

## TELUGO TRANSLATION
By Rama Krishna Perugo

# ఒక బహుమతి II

ఆకాశం ప్రకాశవంతంగా మరియు స్వలింగ సంపర్కం
మంత్రముగ్ధలను చేసే నక్షత్రాలతో రాత్రి బెజ్వెల్
చేయబడింది
చంద్రుడు మరియు దాని అందంగా రూపొందించిన
కందకాలు

దూరం నుండి, చిలిపి క్రికెట్లు చెవులకు ఆహ్లాదకరంగా
ఉంటాయి
తెల్లవారుజాము వరకు విలాసవంతమైన రాత్రిని
సృష్టించడం.
రండి, అందమైన రాత్రి వేడుకుంటుంది
ఆ నీటిని తాగుదాం
సరిచేసే నదుల వైపు నడుస్తుంది

విరిగిన హృదయాలు మరియు ఆత్మలు.

ఓహ్, నిధిని భరిద్దాం

అదృశ్యమైనట్లు అనిపించిన బహుమతి

ఇప్పటికీ శ్వాస మరియు కొనసాగుతోంది

విరిగిన ఆశలు మరియు కలలకు జీవితాన్ని ఇవ్వండి

కోల్పోయిన కోర్సును వంతెన చేయండి మరియు

కోల్పోయిన ఆత్మకు అర్థం కనుగొనండి.

ఓహ్! బహుమతిని నిధిగా ఉంచుకుందాం

అందమైన రాత్రి రండి.

# VIETNAMESE TRANSLATION
## By HONG NGOC CHAU

# MỘT MÓN QUÀ II

Bầu trời sáng rực rỡ và vui vẻ
Đêm được trang hoàng với những sao
Đầy vẻ đam mê và huyễn hoặc
Với bao ánh sáng thật thanh tao

Các rãnh mặt trăng được chế tác
Long lanh ẩn hiện đẹp làm sao
Từ xa tiếng dế gáy đồng vọng
Vui thích bên tai thật ngọt ngào

Tạo một đêm thanh giàu nhạc điệu
Hòa hài giao hưởng đến bình minh
Chúng ta hãy đến cùng đêm đẹp
Hãy đến như đêm thành khẩn xin

Này nhé chúng ta cùng uống nước
Chúng ta cùng đến ngay dòng sông
Đôi tim với khối hồn tan vỡ.
Kho báu tình ta nén tất lòng

Một món quà dường như biến mất
Vẫn đang hít thở, đang sinh tồn
Trao cho cuộc sống những hy vọng
Những ước mơ tan vỡ đáy hồn

Hạn chế bài học xưa đánh mất
Tìm trong ý nghĩa mất linh hồn.
Cho ta chịu đựng quà trân trọng
Đêm tuyệt vời ta đang ngóng trông.

# TRANSLATION

# ON

# A

# GIFT III

# A GIFT III

Petals are artless to the eyes
Dots rule their innermost being and
Forsaken with the aromatic smell
Like falling leaves that are
Diverse in size and shape without their
typical budding point and smell
But its beauty and essence lie from within
And you, a Gift
like
Petals and leaves whose essence
springs from its bosom—

Endless

like water in the ocean
Ceaselessly musing and inspiring
As the beauty from within
Shines the brightest and
Keeps on shining its brightest

## ALBANIAN TRANSLATION
By Sherife Allko

# Një DHURAT III

Petalet janë artistike për sytë
Pikat sundojnë qenien e tyre më të brendshme dhe
I braktisur me erën aromatike
Ashtu si gjethet që bien
Të ndryshme në madhësi dhe formë pa ato
pika tipike e lulëzimit dhe aroma
Por bukuria dhe thelbi i saj qëndrojnë nga brenda
Dhe ju, një dhuratë
si
Petale dhe gjethe thelbi i të cilave
buron nga gjiri i saj -

E pafund

si uji në oqean
Mos pushuar vazhdimisht dhe frymëzues
Si bukuroshja nga brenda
Shndrit më të ndritshme dhe
Vazhdon të shkëlqejë më së miri
Luzviminda

# ASSAMESE TRANSLATION
By Malakshmi Borthakur

## এটি উপহাৰ (৩)

ফুলৰ পাপৰি বিলাক দেখাত সৰল
বিন্দুবিলাকে সিহঁতৰ হৃদয়ৰ গভীৰতম সত্তাত আধিপত্য চলায়
আৰু পৰিত্যক্ত হৈ ৰয় সুগন্ধিযুক্ত পাপৰি বিলাক !
পুনৰ্অংকুৰিত হোৱাৰ সম্ভাৱনাবিহীন,
সুগন্ধিবিহীন সৰাপাত বিলাকৰ দৰে সিহঁত, বিভিন্ন আকৃতিৰ
!
তথাপি সিহঁতৰ নিৰ্যাস নিঃসৰিত হয় অভ্যন্তৰৰ পৰা ।
তুমি মোৰ বাবে এটি উপহাৰ
ফুলৰ পাপৰি আৰু পাতবিলাকৰ দৰে !
যাৰ নিৰ্যাস নিঃসৰিত হয় অভ্যন্তৰৰ পৰা ।

তুমি অনন্ত
সাগৰে বহন কৰা জলৰাশিৰ দৰে !
অবিৰত ভাবে ধ্যানমগ্ন আৰু প্ৰেৰণাদায়ক
তুমি অন্তৰ্মনৰ সৌন্দৰ্যৰ দৰে
যি উজ্জ্বলৰ পৰা উজ্জ্বলতৰ হৈ জিলিকে !

# BENGALI TRANSLATION
## By Queen Sarkar

# একটি উপহার ।।।

পাপড়ি চোখের কাছে অকৃত্রিম হয়

বিন্দু তাদের অভ্যন্তরীণ সত্তা এবং

সুগন্ধযুক্ত গন্ধে ত্যাগ করা

ঝরে পড়া পাতার মতো

এদের বৈচিত্রময়  আকার এর আকৃতি

সাধারণ উদীয়মান এবং  গন্ধ ছাড়া

কিন্তু এর সৌন্দর্য এবং সারাংশ অন্তর থেকে নিহিত

আপনি, একটি এদের মত উপহার

যেমন

পাতা আর পাপড়ি যার সুগন্ধ

বক্ষ থেকে ঝর্ণার মত বেরিয়ে আসে


অবিরাম

সমুদ্রের জলের মতো

নিরলসভাবে সংগীত এবং অনুপ্রেরণা দেয়

যেমন আমাদের ভেতরের সৌন্দর্য

জ্বলজ্বল করে এবং

সারা জীবন জ্বলজ্বল করতে থাকে

# BRAZILIAN TRANSLATION
By Shakil Kalam

## Um presente-3

As pétalas são feias para os olhos,
deixando pontos como sua entidade
interna e folhas caindo sem cheiro.
Sem eles, os caules dos ramos variam em forma e
cor.

Mas sua beleza e essência estão no coração,
Você é como um presente de pétalas e extrato de
folhas.

Descarga primavera-primavera como água do mar
sem fim;
Incansavelmente com música e
inspiração.
Sua beleza interior é a radiação mais
brilhante, portanto, mantém o brilho de sua
radiação.

# DARI TRANSLATION
By Parwez Hashimi

## تحفه دوهم:-

آسمان روشن است و همجنسگرا شب با ستاره ها و سنگرهای زیبایی ساخته شده آن از ستاره های دلربا مجذوب می شود.
از دور ، جیرجیرک های دلپذیر برای گوش خشنود هستند و یک شب آرام و طوفانی تا طلوع آفتاب ایجاد می کنند. بیا شب زیبا با ادعای ،    بگذار آب ما را به رودخانه هایی که ، قلب و روح شکسته را اصلاح می کنند ، بنوشیم. اوه بگذارید تحمل کنیم گنج گنج
هدیه ای که به نظر می رسد ناپدید می شود اما هنوز نفس می کشد و زندگی خود را به امیدها و آرزوهای شکسته ادامه می دهد.

مسیر گمشده را مرتب کنید و به روح گمشده معنی دهید. اوه بگذارید تحمل کنیم که یک هدیه را گنج کنیم ، بیا شب زیبایی استعلام می کند.

# GUJARATI TRANSLATION
By Bhanubhai Patel

# ભેટ III

પાંખડીઓ આંખો માટે કલાહિન છે
બિંદુઓ તેમના આંતરિક અસ્તિત્વ પર
શાસન કરે છે અને સુગંધિત સુવાસથી
ત્યજી પડતા પાંદડાની જેમ જેઓ તેમના
લાક્ષણિક ઉભરતા બિંદુ અને ગંધ વિના કદ અને
આકારમાં વૈવિધ્યસભર પરંતુ તેની સુંદરતા
અને સાર અંદર છે
અને તમે, એક ઉપહાર
પાંદડીઓ અને પાંદડાઓની
જેમ
જેનો સાર તેના ઊર્મિકેન્દ્રમાંથી સ્ફુરે છે ----

અનંત

સમુદ્રમાં પાણીની જેમ
અવિરતપણે ચિંતવન અને પ્રેરણાદાયક
આંતરિક સુંદરતાની જેમ
સૌથી તેજસ્વી ચમક અને
તેની તેજસ્વીતા ચમકતી રહે છે

## PASHTO TRANSLATION
By Parwez Hashimi

# A_دریمه ډالۍ

د ګلونو پاڼې د سترګو د دید لپاره بی نقصه
دي.
په ګل کی تر ټولو دننه حاکمی نقطې چی د
ګل خوشبویي لکه د غورځیدلو پانو په ځیر له
منځه وړي د اندازی او شکل له نظره فرق
لري.
دغه نقطې او معمولي خوشبویي د غوتی
وهلو، خو ښکلا او جوهر يي له دننه خوا څخه
دی او تاسو، هغه تحفه یاست لکه د ګل پاڼې او
هغه پاڼې چی جوهر او ښکلا يي له ځانښ
څخه سرچینه اخلي.
لکه په سمندر کی اوبه بی دمي موسیقي او
الهام بخشه دي.
لکه څنګه چی ښکلا د رڼاوو په منځ څلیږي
او خپلی ځلا ته دوام وركوي.

# PUNJABI TRANSLATION
### By Mohit Katyal

## ਇੱਕ ਉਪਹਾਰ 3

ਫੁੱਲ ਅਖਾਂ ਨੂੰ ਬੇਤੁਕੇ ਲਗਦੇ ਹਨ
ਬਿੰਦੀਆਂ ਉਨ੍ਹਾਂ ਦੇ ਅੰਦਰਲੇ ਜੀਵ ਉਤੇ ਰਾਜ ਕਰਦੀਆਂ ਹਨ
ਉਹ ਖ਼ੁਸ਼ਬੂ ਨੂੰ ਤਿਆਗ ਦਿੰਦੇ ਹਨ
ਡਿੱਗਦੇ ਪੱਤਿਆਂ ਵਾਂਗ
ਅਕਾਰ ਅਤੇ ਸ਼ਕਲ ਵਿਚ ਵੱਖ ਵੱਖ ਨੇ
ਆਮ ਉਭਰਦੇ ਬਿੰਦੁ ਅਤੇ ਗੰਧ ਵੀ ਵੱਖ
ਪਰ ਇਸ ਦੀ ਸੁੰਦਰਤਾ ਅੰਦਰੂਨੀ ਹੈ
ਅਤੇ ਤੂੰ, ਜਿਵੇਂ ਇਸਦਾ ਦਿੱਤਾ ਉਪਹਾਰ

ਫੁੱਲ ਅਤੇ ਪੱਤੇ ਜਿਨ੍ਹਾਂ ਦੇ ਤੱਤ
ਇਸ ਦੀ ਹਿਕ ਤੋਂ ਝੂਲਦੇ ਹਨ

ਬੇਅੰਤ

ਸਮੁੰਦਰ ਦੇ ਪਾਣੀ ਵਾਂਗ
ਬੇਅੰਤ ਸੰਗੀਤ ਅਤੇ ਪ੍ਰੇਰਣਾਦਾਇਕ
ਜਿਵੇਂ ਕਿ ਇਸਦੀ ਅੰਦਰੂਨੀ ਸੁੰਦਰਤਾ
ਚਮਕਦਾਰ ਹੈ
ਇਹਦੇ ਵਾਂਗ ਚਮਕਦਾ ਰਹਿੰਦਾ ਹੈ

<h1 style="text-align:center">SETSWANA TRANSLATION</h1>
By Kenneth Maswabi

<h1 style="text-align:center">Mpho (karolo ya boraro)</h1>

Dithunya ga dina boleng mo tebong ya matlho
Mme diagilwe ka bontlenyane mo boteng jwa tsone
Ditlogeletswe menko ee monate
Jaaka matlhare aa wang mo setlhareng
A farologane ka bophara le dipopego
A ntshitswe ditebego le menko ya tsone
Mme bontle le boleng jwa one boagetswe moteng
Mme wena, o mpho
Fela jaaka matlhare a dithunya le one matlhare tota
Boleng jwa gago bosimologa mo boteng jwa pelo ya
gago
Gosa feleng
Jaaka metsi a lowatle
Gao emise go makatsa le go senola lesedi lwa gago
Bontle jobo tswang mo pelong
Bophatsima mo go feteletseng
Mme botswelela bophatsima

# TAMIL TRANSLATION
By Radhakrishan Krishnan

## ஒரு பரிசு III

இதழ்கள் கண்களுக்கு கலையற்றவை.
புள்ளிகள் அவற்றின் உள்மனதை
ஆளுகின்றன.
மணமில்லாது உதிர்ந்த வெவ்வேறு
விதமான இலைகள் போல
வாடையின்றி முளைக்கும்
திறனின்றிய போதிலும்
இதழ்களின் அழகும் மணமும்
அவைகளின் உட்பொருளே.
அந்த இதழல்கள் போல
உள்ளழகுடைய நீயும் ஒரு பரிசு தான்.
எப்படி இதழ்களின் சாரம் அதன்
இதயத்திலிருந்து எழுவது போல்.
கடலில் உள்ள நீர்த்துளிகள் போல

அளவில்லாமல்
ஊக்கமளிக்கும் உங்கள் மனதின் அழகு
எப்பொழுதுமே பிரகாசிக்கவும்,

# TELUGO TRANSLATION
By Rama Krishna Perugo

## బహుమతి III

రేకులు కళ్ళకు కళలేనివి

చుక్కలు వాటి అంతరంగికతను నియంత్రిస్తాయి మరియు

సుగంధ వాసనతో విడిచిపెట్టండి

పడిపోయే ఆకులు వంటివి

వాటి లేకుండా పరిమాణం మరియు ఆకారంలో

వైవిధ్యమైనది

సాధారణ చిగురించే స్థానం మరియు వాసన

కానీ దాని అందం మరియు సారాంశం లోపలి నుండే

ఉంటాయి

మరియు మీరు, ఒక బహుమతి

వంటి

రేకులు మరియు ఆకులు దీని సారాంశం

దాని టోసోమ్ నుండి బుగ్గలు

అంతులేనిది

సముద్రంలో నీరు వంటిది

నిరంతరాయంగా మ్యూజింగ్ మరియు స్ఫూర్తిదాయకం

లోపల నుండి అందం

ప్రకాశవంతమైన ప్రకాశిస్తుంది మరియు

దాని ప్రకాశవంతమైన మెరుస్తూనే ఉంటుంది

## VIETNAMESE TRANSLATION
### By HONG NGOC CHAU

# MỘT MÓN QUÀ III

Cánh hoa vô hồn trong đáy mắt
Như là dấu chấm ngự trên ngôi
Bên trong bản thể con người họ
Từ bỏ mùi thơm như lá rơi

Đa dạng hình thù và kích thước
Tượng trưng dấu chấm nở bung rồi
Hương thơm không có nhưng hoa đẹp
Bản chất nằm trong sự vật rồi

Một món quà hoa có bản chất
Của mùa xuân tình cảm đầu nguôn
Nước trong của đại dương vô tận
Cảm hứng không ngừng ngầm chảy tuôn

Vẻ đẹp từ bên trong tỏa sáng
Lung linh sáng chói, thật huy hoàng
Vẫn luôn tiếp tục tung tia sáng
Rực rỡ trong không gian sáng choang

# TRANSLATION

# ON

# A

# GIFT IV

# A GIFT IV

The raging storms in life ---
hostile wind that brings sting
raindrops during the cloudiest hours
thunder and lightning rupturing
from the heart breaking.

The storms that gave birth to these rivers
drowning
the broken hearts and lost souls
But a Gift bridles the lost course and
Gives life to the dying soul.

A Gift,  brilliant as a diamond
Life's treasure that is priceless
No storms can dim its luster
perfected through trust and respect
more matured minds and
enduring hearts
can understand

## ALBANIAN TRANSLATION
By Sherife Allko

# NJË DHURAT 4

Stuhitë e tërbuara në jetë ---
erë armiqësore që sjell pickim
pikat e shiut gjatë orëve me re
bubullima dhe shpërthimi i vetëtimës
nga zemra e thyer.

Stuhitë që lindën këta lumenj
mbytja
zemrat e thyera dhe shpirtrat e humbur
Por një Dhuratë bën fre kursin e humbur dhe
I jep jetë shpirtit që vdes.

Një dhuratë, e shkëlqyer si një diamant
Thesari i jetës që është i pavlefshëm
Asnjë stuhi nuk mund ta zbehë shkëlqimin e saj
përsosur përmes besimit dhe respektit
mendje më të pjekura dhe
zemra të qëndrueshme
mund ta kuptoj

# ASSAMESE TRANSLATION
By Malakshmi Borthakur

## এটি উপহাৰ (৪)

জীৱনলৈ অহা প্ৰচণ্ড কালধুমুহা কেইজাক !
খঙাল বতাহজাকে মেঘাচ্ছন্ন সময়খিনিত কটিয়াই আনে
বৰষুণৰ শুং থকা কণিকা বিলাক ।
বজ্ৰপাত আৰু মেঘৰ গৰ্জনবিলাক যেন একোখনি হৃদয় টুকুৰা
টুকুৰ হওঁতে ওলোৱা শব্দহে !

সেই ধুমুহাকেইজাকে প্ৰসৰ কৰিছিল সেই নদী কেইখনক,
য'ত ডুবি গৈছিল ভগ্ন হৃদয় কেইখন আৰু পৰাজিত আত্মা
কেইটা !
কিন্তু এটি উপহাৰে সেই তচনচ হৈ যোৱা শৃংখলাটোক সামৰি
ল'লে,
আৰু সেই মৃতপ্ৰায় আত্মাক পুনৰোজ্জীৱিত কৰিলে ।

এটি উপহাৰ, যি এটুকুৰা হীৰা সদৃশ উজ্জ্বল,
এটি উপহাৰ, যি জীৱনৰ অমূল্য সম্পদ।
কোনো কালধুমুহাই ইয়াৰ উজ্জ্বলতাক ম্লান কৰিব নোৱাৰে !
এটি উপহাৰ, যি বিশ্বাস আৰু সন্মানেৰে পৰিপূৰ্ণ,
যিটো কেৱল এজন পৰিপক্ক আৰু ধৈৰ্য্যশীল ব্যক্তিৰ দ্বাৰাহে
বোধগম্য ।

**BENGALI TRANSLATION**
By Queen Sarkar

# একটি উপহার IV

জীবনের ঝড় ঝাপটা---

বৈরী বাতাস যা ডেকে আনে দংশন

মেঘলা সময়ের মধ্যে বৃষ্টিপাত

বিদ্যুৎ এবং বজ্রপাত

যা ভগ্ন হৃদয়এর থেকে উঠে আসে।


এই ঝড় যা জন্ম দিয়েছে নদীগুলি কে

আজ তাতে ডুবে যাচ্ছে

ভগ্ন হৃদয় এবং হারানো আত্মা

কিন্তু একটি উপহার হারানো আত্মা কে পথ দেখায়

মরে যাওয়া আত্মা কে জীবন দেয়।


একটি উপহার, যা হীরার মত উজ্জ্বল

জীবনের ধন যা অমূল্য

কোনও ঝড় তার দীপ্তি ম্লান করতে পারে না

বিশ্বাস এবং শ্রদ্ধার মাধ্যমে নিখুঁত

আরও পরিপক্ক মন এবং

স্থায়ী হৃদয়

এইটি বুঝতে পারে

# BRAZILIAN TRANSLATION
By Shakil Kalam

## Um presente-4

O vento hostil da vida traz uma tempestade violenta
-
Há muita chuva e trovões durante os dias nublados;
Esse raio quebra a mente das pessoas e se torna
monótono.

O coração do rio, partido pela corrente,
está partido e a alma está perdida.
Mas fecha o caminho e dá vida à alma morta do rio.

Os diamantes brilhantes são um presente
maravilhoso e um bem inestimável para a vida.
Nenhuma tempestade pode diminuir seu brilho.
Através da fé e da reverência, a mente humana é
aperfeiçoada,
Ele ganha maturidade, amplitude e clareza.
Essas pessoas podem ter um assento
permanente no coração

# DARI TRANSLATION
By Parwez Hashimi

تحفه چهارم:_

طوفان های شدید در زندگی ___ باد خصمانه ای که بارانهای باران را در طی ابرترین ساعت ها به همراه دارد

رعد و برق و رعد و برق از شکستن قلب.

او طوفان هایی را به وجود آورد که این رودخانه ها را غرق قلب های شکسته و روح هایشان کرده است

اما یک هدیه مسیر گمشده را آویز می کند و زندگی را به روح در حال مرگ می بخشد.

یک هدیه ، به عنوان یک الماس درخشان گنج زندگی که بی ارزش است هیچ طوفانی نمی تواند درخشش خود را با اعتماد و احترام کامل کند

ذهن های بالغ تر و قلب های ماندگار می توانند درک کنند.

# GUJARATI TRANSLATION
By Bhanubhai Patel

# ભેટ IV

જીવનમાં પ્રચંડ તોફાનો ---
પ્રતિકૂળ પવન જે ડંખ લાવે છે
સઘન વાદળછાયા કલાકો દરમિયાન
વર્ષાબિંદુ હ્રદય તોડી નાખતા
ગાજવીજ અને વીજળી

તોફાનો જેણે આ નદીઓને જન્મ આપ્યો છે
તૂટેલા હ્રદય અને ખોવાયેલા આત્માઓને
ડૂબાડતા
પરંતુ એક ઉપહાર ખોવાયેલા પંથ પર અંકુશ
અને મરનાર આત્માને જીવન આપે છે.

એક ભેટ, હીરાની જેમ તેજસ્વી
જીવનનો ખજાનો જે અમૂલ્ય છે
કોઈ તોફાન તેની ચમકને મંદ કરી શકશે નહીં
વિશ્વાસ અને આદર દ્વારા પરિપૂર્ણ
વધુ પરિપક્વ દિમાગ અને
સહનશીલ હ્રદય
સમજી શકે છે.

# PASHTO TRANSLATION
## By Parwez Hashimi


څلورمه ډالۍ
په ژوند کې تر ټولو زورور طوفانونه_ هغه شدید بادونه چی ځانه
سره باران ولري تر ټولو سختو وریځ ﻟﺮونکو ساعتونو په جريان
کی،تند،برېښناد زړه له ماتوالی څخه.
هغه،هغه طوفانونه منځته راوړي چی دا سيندونه په ماتو زړونو
او ورک شوو روحونو کی غرقوي
خو يوه تحفه ورک شوی مسير څرخوي او مړ شوی روح ته
ژوند ورکوي.
هيڅ طوفان نشي کولی خپل درخشش هر ځان باور باندی پوره
کړي،او بالغ ذهن ته احترام وکړي.


^^^^^^^^^^^^^^^^^^^^^^^^^^^^^^^^^^^^^^


پنځمه ډالۍ
کله چی اسمان ته فکر وکړم،د يوي په زړه پوري ملګرتيا ښکلي
خاطرات ګورم چی د زماني امتحانونو په وړاندی پايدار دي.
ګورم چی د شديد باد پواسطه سرګردانه وریځي سره
راټوليږي(قوي کيږي)او هغه باران اوروي کوم چی روح تازه
کوي.
زه ګورم الوتونکي له خپلي آزادي څخه خوند اخلي،او لوړو
ارتفاعاتو ته الوزي بدون له چی د ژوند مبارزاتو ته فکر
وکړي.
ژوند هغه تحفه ده چی دا بادونه به د هغي له باد لاندی وي.

# PUNJABI TRANSLATION
## By Mohit Katyal

# ਇੱਕ ਉਪਹਾਰ 4

ਜ਼ਿੰਦਗੀ ਵਿਚ ਤੂਫ਼ਾਨ ਆਉਂਦੇ ਹਨ ---
ਗਜਦੀ ਹਵਾ, ਜੋ ਬਿਪਤਾ ਲਿਆਉਂਦੀ ਹੈ
ਬੱਦਲਵਾਈ ਦੇ ਸਮੇਂ ਬਾਰਸ਼
ਜੋ ਟੁੱਟੇ ਦਿਲਾਂ ਵਿੱਚੋਂ
ਰਾਹ ਬਣਾਉਂਦੀ ਹੈ

ਤੂਫ਼ਾਨ ਜਿਨ੍ਹਾਂ ਨੇ ਇਨ੍ਹਾਂ ਨਦੀਆਂ ਨੂੰ ਜਨਮ ਦਿੱਤਾ
ਇਸ ਦੀ ਡੂੰਘਾਈ ਵਿੱਚ ਡੁੱਬ ਰਹੇ ਹਨ
ਇਥੇ ਟੁੱਟੇ ਦਿਲ ਅਤੇ ਗੁੰਮੀਆਂ ਰੂਹਾਂ
ਪਰ ਇੱਕ ਉਪਹਾਰ ਗੁੰਮ ਰਸਤੇ ਨੂੰ ਰਾਹ ਦਿਖਾਦਾਂ ਹੈ
ਮਰਦੀ ਰੂਹਾਂ ਨੂੰ ਸਾਹ ਦਿੰਦਾ ਹੈ.

ਇੱਕ ਉਪਹਾਰ, ਹੀਰੇ ਵਾਂਗ ਚਮਕਦਾਰ
ਜ਼ਿੰਦਗੀ ਦਾ ਖ਼ਜ਼ਾਨਾ ਜੋ ਅਨਮੋਲ ਹੈ
ਕੋਈ ਤੂਫ਼ਾਨ ਇਸਦੀ ਚਮਕ ਨੂੰ ਧੁੰਦਲਾ ਨਹੀਂ ਕਰ ਸਕਦਾ
ਵਿਸ਼ਵਾਸ ਅਤੇ ਸਤਿਕਾਰ ਦੁਆਰਾ ਸੰਪੂਰਨ
ਦਿਲ ਇਸ  ਉਪਹਾਰ ਨੂੰ
ਸਮਝ ਸਕਦਾ ਹੈ

## SETWANA TRANSLATION
By Kenneth Maswabi

# Mpho (karolo ya bone)

Matsubutsubu a botshelo
Diphefo tse dimakatsang dirwele botlhoko
Marotlhodi aa nang ka nako tse dirweleng maru
Dikgadima le tladi di thubega
Gotswa boteng jwa pelo ee thubegileng

Matsubutsubu aa tshotseng dinoka tsa morwalela
Oo hupetsang dipelo tse dibotlhoko le mewa ee
latlhegileng
Mme Mpho e, e tsenya ditomo mo tseleng ee
latlhegileng
Mme e tsenye botshelo mo mowing oo swang

Mpho e, e tletse dimakatso jaaka teemane
Ditshomarelo tsa botshelo tse disenang bokhutlo
Ga gona matsubutsubu aa ka timang lesedi la yone
E thatagaditswe ka bopaki le boamaaruri
Tlhaloganyo tse diitshetletseng
Le pelo tse di iketlileng
Ditla tlhaloganya

# TAMIL TRANSLATION

By Radhakrishan Krishnan

## ஒரு பரிசு IV

வாழ்க்கையில் பொங்கி எழும்
புயல்களும்
கொட்டும் விரோத காற்றுகளும்
மேகமூட்டமான நேரங்களின்
மழைத்துளிகளும்
இதயம் உடைந்து நொறுங்கியதால்
உண்டான இடியும் மின்னலும்
அவைகள் எல்லாம் சேர்ந்து
உண்டாக்கும் வெள்ளத்தில்
மூழ்கிய இதயத்தையும்
ஆத்மாவையும் உயிர்பிப்பது ஒரு பரிசு.
வைரத்தின் போல் பளபளக்கும் பரிசு
விலைமதிர்ப்பற்ற வாழ்க்கையின்
புதையல்
நம்பிக்கை மற்றும் மரியாதையுடன்

பூரணமடைந்த பரிசை எந்த புயல்களும்
அழிக்க முடியாது
அந்த பரிசின் மதிப்பை முதின்ற மனமும்
இதயமும் தான் புரிந்துகொள்ள முடியும்

# TELUGO TRANSLATION
By Rama Krishna Perugo

## బహుమతి IV

జీవితంలో ఉగ్రమైన తుఫానులు ---
స్టింగ్ తెచ్చే శత్రు గాలి
మేఘావృతమైన గంటలలో వర్షపు చినుకులు
ఉరుములు, మెరుపులు చీలిపోతున్నాయి
గుండె పగలగొట్టడం నుండి.

ఈ నదులకు జన్మనిచ్చిన తుఫానులు
మునిగిపోతుంది
విరిగిన హృదయాలు మరియు కోల్పోయిన ఆత్మలు
కానీ బహుమతి కోల్పోయిన కోర్సును వంతెన చేస్తుంది
మరణిస్తున్న ఆత్మకు జీవితాన్ని ఇస్తుంది.

ఒక బహుమతి, వజ్రం వలె తెలివైనది
అమూల్యమైన జీవిత నిధి
ఏ తుఫానులు దాని మెరుపును మసకబారవు

నమ్మకం మరియు గౌరవం ద్వారా పరిపూర్ణత
మరింత పరిణతి చెందిన మనస్సులు మరియు
శాశ్వతమైన హృదయాలు
అర్థం చేసుకోగలదు

# VIETNAMESE TRANSLATION
## By HONG NGOC CHAU
# MỘT MÓN QUÀ IV

Bão tố dữ dằn trong cuộc sống
Gió thù địch mang lại chua cay
Hạt mưa trong buổi nhiều mây nhất
Sấm chớp luân phiên xé góc trời

Từ trái tim yêu từng đổ vỡ
Mà bao giông tố đã khai sinh
Con sông dìm chết tim tan nát
Lạc mất linh hồn kẻ thất tình

Một món quà yêu tuy hạn chế
Mất phương lạc hướng để hồi sinh
Trao cho sự sống hồn gần chết
Quà tặng kim cương sáng rực tình

Kho báu cuộc đời là quý giá
Không giông bão khiến nó mờ đi
Thông qua tin tưởng và tôn trọng
Tâm trí trưởng thành trong phút giây

Chịu đựng trái tim có thể hiểu
Cuộc tình như thể áng mây bay
Có nhiều đau khổ thêm kinh nghiệm
Hạnh phúc về sau thêm đủ đầy

# TRANSLATION

# ON

# A

# GIFT V

# A Gift V

As I gaze upon the sky
I see the beautiful memories of
A wonderful friendship that
Stands through the test of time

I see the wandering clouds
Being pushed by the hostile wind
Resilient and forming a rain
Refreshing to the soul.

I see the birds enjoying their liberty
Soaring at their greater heights
No matter what life's struggle
A Gift will always be the wind beneath their wings.

I see the sun with its brilliant rays
Which continues to shine at its brightest
No matter how strong the storms may be
A Gift will be its strength forever.

# ALBANIAN TRANSLATION
By Sherife Allko

## Një dhuratë V

Ndërsa vështroj qiellin
Unë shoh kujtimet e bukura të
Një miqësi e mrekullueshme që
Qëndron në provën e kohës

Unë shoh retë endacake
Të shtyrë nga era armiqësore
Elastike dhe duke formuar një shi
Freskuese për shpirtin.

Shoh zogjtë duke shijuar lirinë e tyre
Fluturojnë në lartësitë e tyre më të mëdha
Pavarësisht nga lufta e jetës
Një Dhuratë do të jetë gjithmonë era poshtë krahëve
të tyre.

Unë shoh diellin me rrezet e tij të shkëlqyera
E cila vazhdon të shkëlqejë në kohën e saj më të
ndritshme
Pavarësisht se sa të forta mund të jenë stuhitë
Një Dhuratë do të jetë forca e saj përgjithmonë.

# ASSAMESE TRANSLATION
## By Malakshmi Borthakur

# এটি উপহাৰ (৫)

যেতিয়াই মই আকাশলৈ চাওঁ
মই অতুলনীয় বন্ধুত্বৰ সেই মনোৰম স্মৃতি বিলাক দেখা পাওঁ
যি সময়ে লোৱা প্ৰতিটো কঠিন পৰীক্ষাত সফল    !

মই উৰি ফুৰা মেঘবোৰ দেখোঁ
যিবোৰক খঙাল বতাহজাকে ঠেলি পঠিওৱা স্বত্বেও
সিঁহতক প্ৰতিৰোধ কৰি বৰষুণলৈ ৰূপান্তৰিত হয়
আৰু অন্তৰক সজীৱ কৰি তোলে !

মই বান্ধোনবিহীন চৰাইবোৰক আনন্দ কৰা দেখোঁ
দেখা পাওঁ সিঁহতক উৰ্ধগামী হৈ উৰা
জীৱনৰ সংগ্ৰামবিলাক যিমানেই কঠিন নহওক কিয়
এটি উপহাৰে সিঁহতৰ ডেউকাবোৰক   সদায় শক্তি দিব ।

মই দীপ্তিমান সূৰ্যটোক দেখা পাওঁ
যি চিৰকাল উজলি ৰয়
ধুমুহাৰ জাকবোৰ যিমানেই পৰাক্ৰমী নহওক কিয় !
এটি উপহাৰ চিৰকাল তাৰ   শক্তি হৈ থাকিব ।

# BANGLA TRANSLATION
## By Queen Sarkar

# একটি উপহার ৭

আমি যখুন আকাশের দিকে তাকাই
আমি দেখতে পাই সুন্দর স্মৃতি আমাদের
দুর্দান্ত বন্ধুত্ব যা
সময়ের পরীক্ষার মধ্য দিয়ে দাঁড়িয়েছে

আমি ঘুরে বেড়ানো মেঘ দেখি
যা বৈরী বাতাস দ্বারা ধাক্কা খাচ্ছে
আর স্থিতিস্থাপক বৃষ্টিপাত যা
আত্মাকে সতেজ করে তুলছে।

আমি দেখছি পাখিদের স্বাধীনতা উপভোগ করতে
তারা তাদের বৃহত্তর উচ্চতায় উড়ছে
জীবনের সংগ্রাম যাই হোক না কেন
একটি উপহার সর্বদা তাদের ডানার নীচে বাতাসের মত
থাকবে।

আমি সূর্যকে তার উজ্জ্বল রশ্মি দিয়ে দেখছি
যা নিজের উজ্জ্বলতম দিকে জ্বলতে থাকে
ঝড়গুলি যত প্রবলই হোক না কেন
একটি উপহার চিরকাল তার শক্তি হবে।

# BRAZILIAN TRANSLATION
## By Shakil Kalam

## Um presente-5

Eu olho para o céu da vida
Amo relembrar belas lembranças.
Memórias criam uma bela amizade entre nós
Foi feito; Que passou no teste do tempo.

Nuvens se movem no céu com o impulso de um
redemoinho,
Em seguida, as nuvens descem em forma de chuva
sobre a terra.
Essa água purifica e refresca a Alma.

Já vi pássaros desfrutar da liberdade;
E eu vi sua altura e luta pela vida.
O ar sob suas asas será um belo presente.

Eu vejo o sol brilhando com seus raios
brilhantes, cada vez mais brilhantes.
Não importa o quão forte seja a tempestade,
o poder do sol como
um presente para sempre mostra seu poder.

# DARI TRANSLATION
## By Parwez Hashimi


# _:تحفه پنجم


وقتی به آسمان خیره می شوم ، خاطرات زیبا از یک دوستی
در امتحان زمان می ایستد و          شگفت انگیز را می بینم
می بینم که ابر های سرگردان توسط باد خصمانه مقاومت می کنند
و باران را شاداب می کنند.


من می بینم که پرندگان از آزادی خود لذت می برند و در
ارتفاعات بیشترشان بالا می رود بدون توجه به مبارزات زندگی
کدام یک هدیه همیشه باد در زیر آنها خواهد بود.
خورشید را با پرتو های درخشان خود می بینم که همچنان می
درخشد و درخشان می ماند. مهم نیست که طوفان ها چه قدر
ممکن باشند هدیه ای باشد قدرت آن برای همیش خواهد بود.

# GUJARATI TRANSLATION
By Bhanubhai Patel

# ભેટ V

જેમ જેમ હું આકાશ તરફ જોઉં છું
એક અદ્ભુત મિત્રતાની ની સુંદર
યાદો હું જોઉં છું જે સમયની
કસોટીમાં ટકી શકે છે.

હું ભટકતા વાદળોને જોઉં છું
પ્રતિકૂળ પવન દ્વારા દબાણ કરવામાં
આવતા સ્થિતિસ્થાપક અને વરસાદ રચે છે
આત્માને પ્રેરણાદાયક.

હું પક્ષીઓને તેમની સ્વતંત્રતા માણતા જોઉં છું
તેમની મહત્તમ ઊંચાઈએ ચઢતા
જીવનનો સંઘર્ષ કોઈ બાબત નથી
તેમની પાંખોની નીચેનો પવન હંમેશાં ભેટ રહેશે.

હું સૂર્યને તેના તેજસ્વી કિરણો સાથે જોઉં છું
જે તેની મહત્તમ તેજસ્વીતા પર સતત ચમકતા
રહે છે વાવાઝોડું ગમે તેટલું જોરદાર હોય કોઈ દરકાર
નહીં તેની શક્તિ કાયમ માટે તેની ભેટ રહેશે.

# PASHTO TRANSLATION
By Parwez Hashimi

## پنځمه ډالی

کله چی اسمان ته فکر وکړم،د یوي په زړه پوري ملګرتیا ښکلي
خاطرات ګورم چی د زمانۍ امتحانونو په وړاندی پایدار دي.
ګورم چی د شدید باد پواسطه سرګردانه وریځي سره
راتولیږي(قوي کیږي)او  هغه باران اوروي کوم چی روح تازه
کوي.
زه ګورم الوتونکي له خپلي آزادي څخه خوند اخلي،او لوړو
ارتفاعاتو ته الوزي بدون له دی چی د ژوند مبارزاتو ته فکر
وکړي.
ژوند هغه تحفه ده چی دا بادونه به د هغي له باد لاندی وي.

# PUNJABI TRANSLATION
By Mohit Katyal

## ਇੱਕ ਉਪਹਾਰ- 5

ਜਦ ਮੈਂ ਅਸਮਾਨ ਵੱਲ ਵੇਖਦਾ ਹਾਂ
ਮੈਨੂੰ ਖੂਬਸੂਰਤ ਯਾਦਾਂ ਦਿਸਦਿਆਂ ਹਨ
ਇੱਕ ਸ਼ਾਨਦਾਰ ਦੋਸਤੀ ਹੈ ਜੋ
ਸਮੇਂ ਦੀ ਹਰ ਪਰੀਖਿਆ ਲਈ ਤਿਆਰ ਹੈ

ਮੈਂ ਭਟਕਦੇ ਬੱਦਲ ਵੇਖਦਾ ਹਾਂ
ਜਿਸਨੂੰ ਹਵਾ ਨਾਲ ਬਹਾ ਰਹੀ ਹੈ
ਇਹ ਮੀਂਹ ਦਾ ਰੂਪ ਧਾਰਨ ਕਰਕੇ
ਰੂਹ ਨੂੰ ਤਾਜ਼ਗੀ ਦਿੰਦੀ ਹੈ

ਮੈਂ ਪੰਛੀਆਂ ਨੂੰ ਆਜ਼ਾਦੀ ਦਾ ਅਨੰਦ ਮਾਣਦੇ ਵੇਖਦਾ ਹਾਂ
ਉਨ੍ਹਾਂ ਦੀਆਂ ਉੱਚੀਆਂ ਉਚਾਈਆਂ 'ਤੇ ਚੜੁਨਾ
ਇਸ ਨਾਲ ਫ਼ਰਕ ਨਹੀਂ ਪੈਂਦਾ ਜ਼ਿੰਦਗੀ ਦਾ ਕੀ ਸੰਘਰਸ਼ ਹੈ
ਇੱਕ ਉਪਹਾਰ ਹਮੇਸ਼ਾਂ ਉਨ੍ਹਾਂ ਦੇ ਖੰਭਾਂ ਹੇਠ ਹਵਾ ਰਹੇਗਾ.

ਮੈਂ ਸੂਰਜ ਨੂੰ ਉਸਦੀ ਚਮਕਦਾਰ ਕਿਰਨਾਂ ਨਾਲ ਵੇਖਦਾ ਹਾਂ
ਜੋ ਆਪਣੇ ਆਪ ਤੋਂ ਵੀ ਵੱਧ ਚਮਕਦਾ ਹੈ
ਤੂਫਾਨ ਕਿੰਨਾ ਵੀ ਮਜ਼ਬੂਤ ਕਿਉਂ ਨਾ ਹੋਵੇ
ਇਹ ਤੋਹਫਾ, ਹਮੇਸ਼ਾ ਲਈ ਇਸਦੀ ਢਾਲ ਬਣਕੇ ਰਹੇਗਾ

## SETSWANA TRANSLATION
By Kenneth Maswabi

# Mpho (karolo ya botlhano)

Ha ke lebelela loapi
Ke bona dikakanyo tsotlhe tse dintle
Tsa botsalano jo bo kgethegileng
Bo sa tshikinngwe ke dinako

Ke bona maru aa tsamayatsamayang
A kgoromediwa ke diphefo tse dibogale
Mme a le boikobo a nesa pula
A tshela bontle mo mowing

Ke bona dinonyane di itumelela kgololesego ya tsone
Difofela ko godimodimo
Go sa kgatlhalesege gore botshelo bo bokete go le
kahe
Mpho e, ke yone phefo ee fokang ko tlase ga
diphuka tsa tsone

Ke bona letsatsi le galalela ka maranyane a lone
Aa phatsimang ka bokete jo bomakatsang
Le ha matsubutsubu a kanna bothata jo bo kahe
Mpho e, key one dithata tsa lone goya goileng

**TAMIL TRANSLATION**
By  Radhakrishan Krishnan

# ஒரு பரிசு V

நான் வானத்தைப் பார்க்கும்போது
காலத்தின் சோதனைகளில் கலங்காத
ஒர் அற்புதமான நட்பின்
நினைவுகளை காண்கிறேன்

அலைந்து திரிந்த மேகங்களை நான்
காண்கிறேன்
அவைகள் விரோத காற்றால்
தள்ளப்படுவினதால் பொழியும்
மழைதுளிகள்
ஆன்மாவுக்கு புத்துணர்ச்சி
உருவாக்குகிறது

பறவைகள் அதிக உயரத்தில் பறந்து
தங்கள் சுதந்திரத்தை அனுபவிப்பதை
நான் காண்கிறேன்.
வாழ்க்கையின் போராட்டம் எதுவாக
இருந்தாலும்
அந்த பறவைகளின் இறக்கைகள்
கீழே உள்ள காற்று ஒரு பரிசு தான்.

வானத்தில் சூரியன் தன்
பிரகாசமான கதிர்களின் மூலம்
பளபளபதை நான் காண்கிறேன்
புயல்கள் எவ்வளவு வலுவாக
இருந்தாலும்
ஒரு பரிசு என்றென்றும்
அந்த சூரியனின் பலமாக இருக்கும்.

# TELUGO TRANSLATION
By Rama Krishna Perugo

## ఒక బహుమతి V.

నేను ఆకాశం వైపు చూస్తున్నప్పుడు
యొక్క అందమైన జ్ఞాపకాలు నేను చూస్తున్నాను
ఒక అద్భుతమైన స్నేహం
సమయ పరీక్ష ద్వారా నిలుస్తుంది

నేను తిరుగుతున్న మేఘాలను చూస్తున్నాను
శత్రు గాలి ద్వారా నెట్టబడుతోంది
స్థితిస్థాపకంగా మరియు వర్షాన్ని ఏర్పరుస్తుంది
ఆత్మకు రిఫ్రెష్.

పక్షులు వారి స్వేచ్చను ఆస్వాదించడాన్ని నేను
చూస్తున్నాను
వారి ఎక్కువ ఎత్తులో పెరుగుతుంది
జీవిత పోరాటం ఎలా ఉన్నా
బహుమతి ఎల్లప్పుడూ వారి రెక్కల క్రింద గాలి ఉంటుంది.

నేను సూర్యుడిని దాని అద్భుతమైన కిరణాలతో
చూస్తున్నాను
ఇది దాని ప్రకాశవంతమైన వద్ద ప్రకాశిస్తూనే ఉంది
తుఫానులు ఎంత బలంగా ఉన్నా
బహుమతి ఎప్పటికీ దాని బలం అవుతుంది.

# VIETNAMESE TRANSLATION
## By HONG NGOC CHAU

# MỘT MÓN QUÀ V

Đăm đăm tôi ngắm bầu trời rộng
Tôi thấy đẹp sao kỷ niệm xưa
Tình bạn tuyệt vời qua thử thách
Qua thời gian đội nắng che mưa

Tôi thấy đám mây như lãng tử
Lang thang theo gió hình thành mưa
Gió là thù nghịch gom mây tạo
Làm mát tâm hồn nắng giữa trưa

Tôi thấy những con chim tận hưởng
Tự do bay lượn trên không trung
Vút lên mức độ cao hơn hết
Không có đấu tranh đời nói chung

Quà tặng luôn là đôi cánh chúng
Gió nâng đôi cánh chim bay lên
Mặt trời tôi thấy đang say nắng
Tỏa sáng đại dương cả đất liền

Không có vấn đề dù bão mạnh
Món quà sức mạnh là thiêng liêng
Ban cho muôn vật hòa hài sống
Sướng khổ luân phiên lẽ tự nhiên

# DEDICATED POEMS

# Pen Sisters
Ayo Gutierrez

We were birthed tinkering with the embers of
innocence
Oh! This intimacy with words contained in our bated
breaths
Bobbing against waves of our consciousness
Others see the Void, pitch black and cavernous
But we see the cerulean clouds and dandelions, past
the discombobulated weather
...Light transmuting from an unknown source,
illuminating gossamer scarves knitted by a fog— we
reveal our vulnerabilities: uneasy alignments,
dwindling patterns.
Creation, not perfection: must we ever abandon our
wrinkled passion?
It is impossible to get over the idea of returning to
Ithaca:
There was never a concession to unfold, still...
But alas, the truth is made known
The truth is made known.
Nota Bene
Dear sister, exhaustion is a cheap price vis a vis the
masterpiece to unlock.

# A TIME FOR EVERYTHING
Joel P. Ilao
Philippines

Let not the dawning day
be felt like the end of a hard day's work;
Let not the night for rest, be used for toil;
There's a time for everything,
for work and for rest,
a time to start and a time to end;
A time to continue and a time to pause;
A time to rise and a time to fall;
But life is like a meandering brook,
with its twists and turns;
No matter the season,
it continues to flow;
Fallen leaves are wise to ride the steady stream;
their golden days, once green,
mirror the ephemeral and a reminder;
That all belong to a tapestry of unique patches,
brought together by a common nature;
of existence and of being,
unique yet belonging,
to a grand design that looks random;
from eyes that see at close,
yet perfectly and
PURPOSELY PLACED BY AN ARTISTIC
MASTER.

# THE INDELIBLE ONE
Zaldy F. Perez
Philippines


I am mesmerized by your name,
Glamorously painted with fame.
Undeniably a strong woman,
Like nobody else can.

Captivated with your smiles,
Truly fascinating by miles.
Your untiring attitude,
Giving shines that elude.

The magic of your love,
Free and lovely as a dove.
Truly a gift to everyone,
Always and will never be gone.

You are truly a star,
Beautifully beaming from afar.
You have a genuine heart,
Revealingly a work of art.

Time can define you,
In your perspective view.
Strength in your inner core,
You are you and much more.

# IN YOUR JOURNEY
Jomar P. Galapate
Philippines

In your journey
I will be your biggest fan.
Praying for your continued success
A complete collection of your books
Refreshes and inspires my soul
In the remaining days of my life
I pledge my support
To be with your all the way
In whatever journey you are taking in

# YOU ARE A GIFT
Brenda Mohammed
Trinidad and Tobago

 If someone told you are not valuable
Do not allow them to burst your bubble.
You are a gift, there's nothing you lack.
Please do not hold yourself back.

Go ahead and light up the world.
Move forward and watch your life unfold.
Love yourself and to yourself be true.
Search for the massive treasure within you.

Don't compare yourself with another.
Life's not a competition, why bother?
You're extraordinary, don't believe otherwise.
Your life is surely worth living, be wise.

# She Is Luz

Shailesh Veer
India

People-
who are full of enthusiasm,
and always think good for everyone,
She is one of them.

People-
who use their energy positively,
and achieve fame in society by their actions,
She is one of them.

People-
who give a new direction to their lives with hard
work,
and are the reason
for the happiness of others,
She is one of them.

Do you know
who is she?
She is a wonderful human being.
She is a beautiful artist.
She is a prolific poetess.
She is Luz.

Do you know Luz?
Yes! Luz is
Luzviminda Gabato Rivera.

# SHE IS A STAR

Lilian Woo
Malaysia


A star is born
In October
She develops the bond
With all her readers

Through her poetic journey
She creates wonders
With her amazing poetry
Her name is as hot as summer

An energetic and beautiful lady
Her books give unique pleasure
Her dreams of destiny
Materialized with rapture.

## SAINO ( micro poem )

Khemlal Pokhrel
Damak 5, Jhapa ( Nepal)

Please go ahead with high mirth!
The radiant light is focused now!!
The literary dawn shall kiss you!!!

This 7-8-9 syllabled poetical rendering
is for Luzviminda, a poet of repute from
oriental world.

## Haiku for Luzviminda

Annie Johnson

You are a poet.
A talented young woman;
Lovely to behold.

## My best gift
Vandana Sudheesh
India


You came to my world as a beloved sister.
With an attire of happiness, the mesmerizing gesture
You told me things I could learn better.
With the alphabets of motivation as a letter
You showered the blessings upon me that glitter.
As a friend to unlock the shapeless fetter

I thank God for all the plaudits you received a
success.
To play an infinite game in this process.
You are a human with values of life in excess.
With beautiful stars in strength, you mixes.
You proved to have relationships without taxes.
Owned a heart beneath the body that fixes.

# William Thomas Fearby
**Great Britain**

Happy birthday to you my dearest, dearest friend
I hope the feelings this day brings never ever ends
Nothing is too good for you a lovely person thru and
thru
I wish I could bottle up all my love I would send it all
to you
I know this day is special and hope you get what you
desire
A bottle of cheer and a lovely meal in front of an open
fire
And that the memory of this wonderful day forever
lingers on
And stays with you forever when this day has finally
gone

# ACROSTIC
## Chimi Rinzin
## Bhutan

**L:** Legendary being with
**U:** Unassuming
**Z:** Zeal,
**V:** Viable to survive
**I:** Infinite
**M:** Moments of
**I:** Impeccable
**N:** Noteworthiness,
**D:** Diligent and
**A:** Affable natured,
**G:** Gifted with
**A:** Assets to
**B:** Bolster,
**A:** A person of
**T:** Tact,
**O:** Opportune and
**R:** Responsible who is
**I:** Indefatigable,
**V:** Values
**E:** Eternal
**R:** Respect for
**A:** All with simplicity.

**K. Radhakrishnan**
**India**

In her friendship, I found a treasure,
Her kindness can't be put in to measure,
Her friendship has brought abundant pleasure,
Luzviminda, dear friend of benevolent nature.

She is the one with a heart of gold,
That's what I pleasantly found out,
It remains warm when exposed to cold,
Because of the love and compassion it holds.

Her friends affirm her heart is of gold,
That reflects love in million folds,
Nourished by kindness and goodness,
Blessed with grace and brightness.

Sans hatred and untouched by fury,
Unrestrained in love in all its glory,
A heart of gold free from grips of misery,
Holds million tons of gold in its treasury.
Bigger heart even the sky can't enfold,
Luzviminda's heart can never grow old
Her golden heart has ample space,
It holds only love, like a flower vase.

Happy birthday to a poetess of eminence,
Her verses bring joy in abundance,
May her spirit shine in wondrous excellence
In the poetic world, her presence make difference,

**David Wagoner**
**United States of America**

When the wild horses recognize a writer
who knows the blue sky
they listen to poems to prize.
They bow to her with a sigh.
Happy Birthday, Luzviminda Gabato Rivera
 May your birthday be like a herd of beautiful horses,
hard to pick the best moment of all the ones that
pass.

# About

# The

# Music Piece

# MUSIC PIECE *of* A Gift

page 2 of 2

# A GIFT

A GIFT
Guitar Chords
Introduction:
G - D - A - A7 - D, G A
D -
Stanzas:
D F#m - G A - D -
A - D -
G - D - G A - D7 -
Bridge:
G - D - F#m G - A -
G - D F#m - G D - A
D7 -
Chorus:
G - D - A - D7 -
G - D - A - A7 - D, G A
D -
Repeat Stanza,
Bridge and Chorus
Coda:
G - D - A - A7 - D, G A
D -

# About

# The

# Author

# LUZVIMINDA GABATO RIVERA

**Luzviminda Gabato Rivera** is from the Philippines. She is a multi – awarded and bestselling author, an excellent international journal reviewer and multi-awarded researcher.

She finished her postgraduate's courses with academic distinction and academic excellence award such as the Doctor of Public Administration (her 6th degree) and took up units leading to a Bachelor of Law.

She has published five books namely: ***A Gift*** , ***A Gift II*** , composed of 71 poems and translations of her A Gift in 5 series to 23 languages of 17 countries, , ***Crossroads II: A Poets Life Journey*** *—4<sup>th</sup>* Anthology of Motivational Strips composed of 83 World's Best Poets which became Amazon and ***A Memoir of Love*** *— A Quadrilingual ( English, Italian, Frencch and Spanish) in various poetic forms (free verse, haiku, rhyme scheme, sonnet and tanka)* and ***Love Spell —*** A Collection of Sonnets in Asian and European Languages. All five books became rank 1 among bestsellers in Amazon. ***Poets Unify World*** – 6th Anthology of Motivational Strips will be published before the year ends. In addition, her poems have been published in international E-Zines and magazines.

She has received multiple recognitions and the latest is for her literary excellence at par with global standards by Motivational Strips and Gujarat Sahitya Academy of India and 50th Independence Day of Nigeria by Inked with Magic. She also placed first in Southeast Asian Intercontinental Poetry Award as a posthumous tribute to the great poet Kairat Duissenov Parman by Hispanumondial Union of Writers and of the 93 poets chosen in the Motivational Strips Anthology for Kairat.

She serves as the Administrator for Philippine Office of Motivational Strips and an approving editor of Bharath Vision website magazine based in India.

# BIOGRAPHY

# OF

# PHILIPPINES

# TRANSLATORS

# John-John J. Flores
Pangasinan Language Translator

John-John J. Flores is a graduate of Doctor of Philosophy in Language Teaching and a native of Pangasinan. He became an active member of 'Ulupan na Pansiansiay Salitay Pangasinan' (Association of Lasting Pangasinan Language) back in college. He is presently serving as Head Teacher at Tarlac City Schools Division. He is a writer, researcher, and journalism speaker. This memoir is considered one of the best avenues to preserve, value, and propagate native languages like Pangasinan.

# Zaldy F. Perez

Tagalog LanguageTranslator

Zaldy F. Perez is a licensed teacher. He is currently teaching at Maliwalo Central Elementary School, Tarlac City Schools Division. He loves to write poems, songs, jingles and even school, district and municipal hymn. He is always invited in the barangay, school and municipal events as one of the judges. "Makata" is always associated in his name because of his passion and dedication in writing.

# BIOGRAPHY

# OF

# INTERNATIONAL

# TRANSLATORS

# Sheriffe Allko
Albanian Language Translator

Sheriffe Allko started at an early age in her passion for writing. She was born in the city of Librazhd, Albania and now lives in Tirana, Albania. After finishing eighth grade and high school, she started higher studies at the Faculty of Economics. Sheriffe is married and has two children.

## Malakshmi Borthakur
Assamese Language Translator

Malakshmi Borthakur is a multilingual poet, short story writer and translator from India. She has won many international and governmental laurels such as the Certificate of Honour by Motivational Strips and Gujarat Sahitya Akademy (under State Government of Gujarat, India)  on 15th August 2020, World Award For Literary Excellence 2019-2020 from the Government of Peru,  Order of Shakespeare Medal and Global Literature Guardian 2019-2020 from Motivational Strips. Malakshmi also won the World Laureate in Literature 2018, 'World Poetic Star 2019, and Altyn Kalam-Golden Pen from World Nations Writers' Union (WNWU) Kazakhstan. Malakshmi Borthakur is a gold categorized member of Motivational Strips - the world's most active writers forum and an Administrator of its affiliate, 'How To Write  For Success' forum.

## Queen Sarkar
Bengali Translator

Dr. Queen Sarkar is a multilingual poet, an academician, a reviewer, and a translator based in Ranchi, Jharkhand, India. She is currently working as an Assistant Professor in the University Department of English at Ranchi University. She has also been impanelled as an Academic counselor in IGNOU. Sarkar has done her Ph.D. from IIT Kharagpur. Her review articles, poems, and research papers have been published in reputed international journals and anthologies. Dr. Sarkar has been honored by Gujarat Sahitya Akademy and Motivational Strips "for showing literary excellence at par with global standards." She has been appointed as the "Ambassador of Good Will Seeds of Youth XXI Century, India by United Nations of Letters-Uniletras." Sarkar is also the Ambassador of Peace for Switzerland/France. Sarkar is also a bonafide member of the World Nations Writers' Union Kazakhstan.

# Islam Kalam
Brazilian Translator

Root Finder poet Shakil Kalam from Bangladesh received a Master's Degree in Governance Studies from the University of Dhaka. He is known as Central Banker, Corporate Governance Specialist, Child-Litterateur, writer, and Researcher. He has tried to discuss various inconsistencies, inequalities, disillusion, hypocrisy, and human suffering, and the degradation of human moral and social values in his writings. He has been writing stories, poems, rhymes, essays, columns. He relentlessly tried to grasp the Liberation War of Bangladesh, and it also brought diversity in his writings. He published 30 books. He participated in the seminar, symposium, and conferences in various countries such as India, Pakistan, Bhutan, Dubai, Thailand, Singapore, and Malaysia. He is the honorary fellow of the Social Development Research Foundation.

# Parwez Hashimi

Parwez Hashimi is a native of Nangarhar Afghanistan and currently living in Kabul, Afghanistan.

He earned certificates from educational centers such as Diploma in English from the International Educational Center in 2015 and an English Teacher in Ashna Educational Centers in 2016-2018.

He is a polio vaccine volunteer worker and Young Muslims against Corona Virus and currently a medical student at Nangarhar Medical Faculty.

# Bhanubhai Patel

Gujarati Language Translator

Bhanubhai Patel is from Ahmedabad (Gujarat), who is a medical doctor and ex-convict. He has served the Gujarat Government established by Dr. Babasaheb Ambedkar Open University as a consultant. He has done an intensive study in and out of prison. He has set a world record of 54 degrees, diplomas, and certificates, which is recorded in Limca Book of Records, Asia Book of Records, Unique Word Record, India Book of Records, and Universal Record Forum. This memoir is an unforgettable stepping stone to his rare and inspiring prison experiences and academic achievement journey.

## Mohit Katyal
Punjabi Language Translator

Mohit Katyal pens from his life experiences. He has been honoured by Gujrat Sahitya Akademi and Motivational Strips for his contribution in literature. He bagged a position at the University level for "A Phenomenal Woman". Mohit Katyal is now working as a Web Developer and a translator for a renowned poetess.

# Kenneth Maswabi
## Setswana Language Translator

Dr. Kenneth Maswabi is from Botswana, Africa. He is a medical doctor by profession and has been writing poems for a while. His poems were published in various international magazines and e-zines. It has been a challenge to translate the A Gift poems in Setswana but he did it with flying colors.

# K. Radhakrishnan
Tamil Language Translator

K.Radhakrishnan lives in Bhopal city, India. He is a risk manager by profession. He has a passion for writing poetry. LULU PRESS, USA published his first poetry book Reflection of Soul. VISHWABHARATI RESEARCH CENTRE published his second book, Eruption of Bottled Up Emotions. His third book, *Moods in Motion* and his fourth book *Dazzling Dance of Poesy*, has been published by AABS PUBLICATION HOUSE, Kolkata. He has contributed to many international poetry anthologies. He has also won many poetry contests. His poems are regularly featured in international poetry sites such as the DESTINY POETS UK, ATUNIS POETRY, SPILLWORDS, BHARATHVISION and many more. The poet has been honored by Motivational Strips and Gujarat Sahitya Academy for literary excellence at par with global standards.

## Ram Krisma Perugo
Telugo Translator

Poet Laureate Dr. Perugu Ramakrishna (1960) is a widely published, widely traveled, multi-award-winning haiku poet, translator, editor, and a retired tax officer. He has about 25 published works in multiple genres. He visited many countries for presenting poetry and was a featured poet in several prestigious journals and global organisations.

# Hong Ngoc Chau
Vietnamese Translator

Nguyen Chau Ngoc Doan Chinh is from Vietnam and writes HONG NGOC CHAU and NGUYEN CHINH under the pen names. She finished her Master of Education at Vietnam University.

She was awarded the following: DIPLOMA: World Literary Prize World poetic Star 2019; Diploma of II ND Level "Temirqazyq – the Best Poet – Writer of the World, 2019", Gold category member in Motivational Strip, Premio Mundial A La Excelencia Literaria 2019-2020 and Copper cross of The World Union Of Poets for promotion of art 2020.

She published the book *Vietnamese Contemporary Poetry (Volume 1)*, *The Road to the True Heart*, *Pitiable or Blâmable*, and many printed works in newspapers, magazines, and general publications.

# Editor

Ayo Gutierrez

**Ayo Gutierrez** is an international book coach and an Amazon bestselling author. She is also a professional speaker, TV personality, and entrepreneur. She owns GMGA Publishing.

Ayo authored *Yearnings* and co-authored several poetry anthologies and motivational books. When not writing, she enjoys traveling, hosting live Facebook interviews, playing the piano, and teaching poetry to her four children.

She was interviewed live on CNN News Philippines hosted by Rico Hizon due to the international success of her motivational book entitled Chooseday: Life is a Matter of Choice.

# Illustrator

# Kenneth Furnace

Kenneth was born in Los Angeles but now resides in a small town in Oklahoma. He is a veteran of the Army and enjoys being a homebody. He has a wife and three fur kids.

# Music Artist

Noven Perez Cadiang a.k.a. Beetnoven Tchainovsky is from the Philippines. He is a music composer and arranger; some of his works are town hymns and school hymns. He is also a drum and lyre corps trainer, a resident judge in different fields of music like chorale competitions, vocal solo, music writing competition, piano teacher, choir director and a church organist. He has participated in various international choir directors' conference

# Foreword

# and

# Introduction

# Writers

## Shiju H. Pallithazheth

Shiju H. Pallithazheth is a multi-genre, bestselling author of Katashi Tales & The Ghost Wisdom. Author Shiju is the founder of Motivational Strips, the world's most active writers' forum. He additionally handles presidential roles in world's top two writers' unions namely World Nations Writers Union and Union Hispanomundial De Escritores. He is also the Global Advisor of Lasosyasyon Lar Sans Frontyer (Government of Seychelles Literary board). He is respected worldwide as a literary mentor, writers' coach, and motivational speaker. He is currently based in Sultanate of Oman.

## Corina Junghiatu

Corina Junghiatu was born in Romania. She has written and published two books of poetry: "Exile in The Light" and "The Ritual Of A Sunrise". Corina is Publication Coordinator of Motivational Strips, World's Most Active Writers Forum.

She is a Platinum category member in Motivational Strips, as well as an Administrator for Motivational Strips in Romania zone and a Chief Advisor of World Nations Writers' Union Kazakhstan.

# Book

# Reviewers

**Magie F-V Vijay-Kumar**

She was born in the Republic of Seychelles. She is the Chief Editor /Chief Director of the publication of SIPAY Global Literature Journal, Regional Director of Motivational Strips and Chief Representative for World Nations Writers Union for South East Africa /Central Asia, Chief Consultant for three Government Literature Associations, LLSF, Congo, and Rodrigues. She garners various international awards and Literature Arts Award from Seychelles Government for 2017-2019. She holds the PEACOCK oPINION of Superior Quality in Motivational Strips.

She was awarded the PARAGON OF HOPE from Radio/TV CANADA and HERA FOUNDATION if New York was in July 2020. In August 2020, WCHHD ACADEMIC BOARD OF DIRECTORS -GHANA appointed her in this board. In April 2020, BBC NEWS - UK interviewed her about her life as a poet in Seychelles

She has published 31 poetry anthologies to date

# WILLIAM THOMAS FEARBY

William Thomas Fearby is from Burmingham, England, Great Britain.  He is the founder of Poems of Life. He has been writing for seven years, mainly poetry. His poems had been published in various publications and poetry groups, international magazines and e-zines.

## Dr. Shailesh Gupta Veer

Dr. Shailesh Gupta Veer is an Indian poet. He is a bilingual who writes in English & Hindi. He has a Ph.D. in Archaeology. He has edited about a dozen literary books and several magazines. He is also a reviewer and promoter of poetry. He was declared as the Literary Icon in December 2018 by a TV program called "You and Literature Today" from Nigeria.

# K. Radhakrishnan

K.Radhakrishnan lives in Bhopal city, India. He is a risk manager by profession. He has a passion for writing poetry. LULU PRESS, USA published his first poetry book Reflection of Soul. VISHWABHARATI RESEARCH CENTRE published his second book, Eruption of Bottled Up Emotions. His third book, *Moods in Motion* and his fourth book *Dazzling Dance of Poesy*, has been published by AABS PUBLICATION HOUSE, Kolkata. He has contributed to many international poetry anthologies. He has also won many poetry contests. His poems are regularly featured in international poetry sites such as the DESTINY POETS UK, ATUNIS POETRY, SPILLWORDS, BHARATHVISION and many more. The poet has been honored by Motivational Strips and Gujarat Sahitya Academy for literary excellence at par with global standards.

## LISA JOY TOMEY

Lisa believes in life-long learning and tender, loving care of one's work. Her chapbook, Heart Sounds was published in 2018. She has been in two anthologies and several publications including Wolff Poetry Literary Magazine. An editor for Fine Lines Literary Journal, she also works with poets privately. She is currently creating an anthology "Heart Beats" which is slated for publication in 2021. Read her poems on The Prolific Pulse https://prolificpulse.blog/ and enjoy her Prolific Pulse Poetry Podcast https://anchor.fm/lisa-tomey.

# JYOTI NAIR

Jyoti Nair is a quintessential Learning and Development Professional, presently, she works for a top notch Indian MNC as the Capability Development Manager for multiple HR Business Units, where she partners to foster and accelerate transformation momentum for Center of Excellence (COE). She has won several accolades for her literary pursuits, she believes in incessantly whetting her writing skills, and traversing new learning bends each day. Way forward, she aims to harness the power of her pen, championing for the eradication of social stigma around mental illness, for upliftment of victims of domestic violence and for curbing blatant incidents of child abuse.

# Books

# and

# Facebook Pages

# Of

# Luzviminda G. Rivera

## AUTHOR:

A Gift – January 26, 2020 released in Amazon

A Gift II – May 5, 2020 released in Amazon

A Memoir of Love – August 31,2020 released in Amazon

Love Spell –October 27, 2020 released in Amazon

A Gift III – November  27, 2020 released in Amazon


## Publisher/Compiler:

Crossroads – A Poet's Journey
              July 3, 2020 released on Amazon


## INVITATION

If you enjoyed this book or somehow touched your life. Please contact me


Tel. No. +63 09175147038
Email address: :riveraluz71@yahoo.com

## FOLLOW LUZ!

Amazon Author Central – amazon.com./author/luzvimindarivea

## FB PAGES

PoeticMind – www.facebook.com/PoeticMindbyLuzRivera

Research Enthusiasts and Developers (READ) – www.facebook.com/READbyLuzRivera

Wonderful Creations – www.facebook,.com/WonderfulCreationsbyLuzRivera

Fashionate www.facebook.com/fashionatebyLuzRivera

A Gift www.facebook.com/AGiftbyLuzRivera

Crossroads: A Poet's Journey www.facebook.com/CrossroadsbyLuzRivera

Soulful Poetry www.facebook.com/SoulfulPoetrybyLuzRivera

Poets Unify World www.facebook.com/PoetsUnifyWorldbyLuzRivera